A Treasury of Iowa Tales

A Treasury of Iowa Tales

Webb Garrison

with Janice Beck Stock

RUTLEDGE HILL PRESS®
Nashville, Tennessee
A Thomas Nelson Company

Published by Rutledge Hill Press, a Thomas Nelson Company, P.O. Box 141000, Nashville, Tennessee 37214.

Iowa (*It's A Beautiful Name*), by Meredith Wilson © 1946 (Renewed) Variety Music. All Rights controlled and administered by EMI Miller Catalog Inc. All rights reserved. Used by permission. WARNER BROS. PUBLICATIONS U.S. INC., Miami, FL 33014. [p.118]

Library of Congress Cataloging-in-Publication Data

Garrison, Webb
    A treasury of Iowa tales / Webb Garrison.
      p. cm.
    Includes bibliographical references (p.) and index.
    ISBN 1-55853-751-1
      1. Iowa—History--Anecdotes. 2.Iowa—Biography—Anecdotes. I. Title.
    F621.6.G37 1999
    920.0777—dc21
    [B]   99-050170

Printed in the United States of America

1 2 3 4 5 6 7 8 9—04 03 02 01 00

Contents

Preface

During a nationally televised documentary, a commentator briefly turned his attention to Iowa. "This rock-ribbed Republican state," he commented, "is a bastion of midwestern conservatism that is noted chiefly for its production of corn, hogs, and soybeans." His interest in the state and his knowledge of it probably consisted of snippets from the most recent political joust to become national news.

Viewed from Boston Common or from the steps of Independence Hall in Philadelphia, one of the most prominent features of the Hawkeye State is its age. John Carver, first governor of the Plymouth Colony that was later absorbed into Massachusetts, served a one year term. He took office in 1620, a full generation before French trappers observed the Native Americans in the vast region that included Iowa. Gen. James Oglethorpe later led a band of impoverished Londoners to "a haven in the west" that became Savannah, Georgia. The youngest colony to rebel, Georgia was founded two generations before Jacques Marquette and Louis Jolliet first laid eyes on Iowa from the river boat in which they were traveling.

Iowa's relative youth as a state may account for the fact that its "rock-ribbed conservative citizens" have led the nation in one endeavor after another. There's no need to enumerate some of the many fields in which Iowans have been first in the world, since a representative sampling of these appears in chapter eighteen.

Rutledge Hill Press in Nashville, Tennessee, has issued collections of historical non-fiction for about one-fifth of the states that make up today's U.S.A. Nine out of these ten books carry my name on the title page and the spine, and of these I have to tell you that *Iowa* is at or close to the top in reader interest. The territory and then the state served for years as a mecca for easterners with ambition and wanderlust; then, a relatively brief period followed in which the state was the jumping off point for Salt Lake City and other points far to the West. In addition to native-born Iowans, who are amazingly varied in their goals and accomplishments, the state has harbored for a period a large number of men and women who cut wide swaths through the eras in which they flourished.

All of which means that despite the diversity of accounts offered in these pages, a lot of memorable folk are missing. There's nary a word about the Clinton native who wowed London despite being considered a mediocre actress. Maybe citizens of what was then the largest city in the world couldn't help blinking when they caught a glimpse of some of the gems bestowed upon Lillian Russell by Diamond Jim Brady. A sturdy son of Ames got his start as a professional baseball player; if he were alive today, Billy Sunday would make nearly all television evangelists look like beginners just learning about the medium. Alas, Sunday gets no more space here than does Russell.

Truth of the matter is, so many life-long and part-time Iowans have had such interesting lives that no small book can deal with more than a fraction of them. I very much hope that your appetite will be whetted by the vignettes you find here. If that's the case, strike out on your own to learn more about U.S. Secretary of War William Belknap, labor leader John L. Lewis, Supreme Court justice Samuel F. Miller, and the Des Moines publisher who conceived the notion—widely considered to be cockeyed—that Americans in general hanker for better homes and gardens. By all means scan accounts about some imports who came from elsewhere, some exports who left voluntarily or under duress, and such part-part-timers as educator Horace Mann and a fellow who called himself Mark Twain. Even the president of the Confederate States of America spent a fruitful period in Iowa, and the state that never failed to meet its manpower quota in the Civil War was the birthplace of Confederate general Lawrence L. Ross.

To find out more about the people who put the state of tall corn on the intellectual, scientific, and agricultural maps, delve into the Internet and explore the resources of your local library.

Once you get started, you'll find it hard to quit in your quest for true-life stories of such persons as explorer Zebulon Pike; politician Harry Hopkins, who was behind the scenes in practically every aspect of Franklin D. Roosevelt's New Deal; and scientist James A. Van Allen, who helped to lay the foundation for our leap into outer space. For all those who love history or Iowa or both, make Iowa and Iowans top on your list of pursuits.

Part 1
Illusion and Disillusion

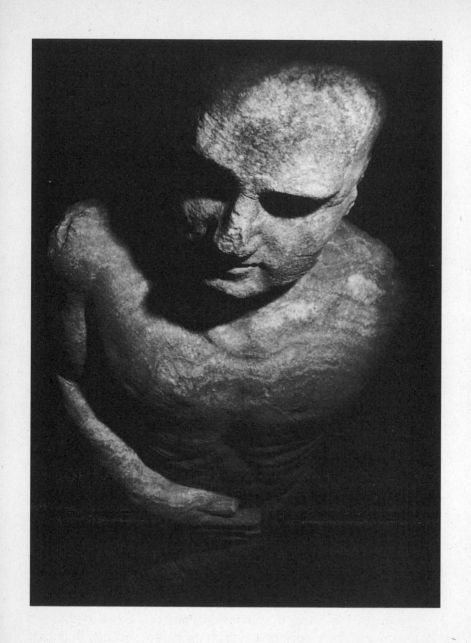

1
Fort Dodge

Gypsum Giant

William "Stub" Newel of Onondaga County, New York, told neighbors his well was drying up. On October 16, 1869, in the village of Cardiff, he found two laborers willing to dig him a new well. Probably using a dowsing rod—a forked branch widely believed to twitch suddenly when properly held above underground water—he located the spot where they were to dig. Long before noon, a shovel hit something big and hard. Newel was called to the site where he directed excavation of a ten-foot figure that he said seemed to be a nude giant in pain.

A hastily erected fence, complete with a gate and a handmade sign that said "ADMISSION 50¢," was in place within hours. Word about Newel's incredible find spread like wildfire. Before dark on the same day, over a thousand people forked over a half dollar in order to get a peek at the giant lying in the rectangular hole that seemed to some "like a huge coffin about five feet deep."

By the middle of the following week, the admission charge had doubled and excursion coaches began making special trips from Syracuse. Front page stories in newspapers detailed the find and offered a variety of speculations about the origin of the statue. The steady stream of excited visitors was originally from Syracuse and the surrounding areas but soon began to include notables who came from a distance.

Henry A. Ward was from Rochester and owned an established museum. He took only one brief look before hinting that he'd very much like to exhibit the giant in his place of business, but Stub shook his head vigorously. "You'll have to talk to my cousin," he mumbled.

Many people came to the farm to examine the giant and offer their theory. Lewis Morgan, a noted regional expert on Indians, admitted he had no idea whether or not Newel had stumbled upon a splendid representation of a god worshipped by Native Americans. An Onondaga Indian insisted, however, that the giant could not be a statue of a god. He believed it was possibly an ancient human that stumbled into a pit dug by his ancestors as a trap for big animals. By the time state geologist James Hall arrived, the find on the Newel farm close to the little settlement of Cardiff was being called the Cardiff Giant and was hailed as a petrified, oversized human.

The crowd of eager visitors buzzed with word that the chancellor of the state university would soon arrive from Albany. John V. S. Pruyn was given a complimentary pass, and onlookers opened a path so he could go directly to "the grave site." Pruyn was still gaping when Alexander McWhorter, a specialist in antiquities, arrived from Harvard. After an hour of looking from every perspective, the scholar gained permission to climb into the pit for a closer look. Emerging with gleaming eyes, he announced to no one in particular: "I'm all but positive that the statue includes some Phoenician characters, plus the symbol those people used for the Deity!" If correct, his verdict would mean that a carving executed many centuries earlier had been transported all the way to the New World by unknown people for no logical reason.

Some persons who paid daily visits to the site of the discovery knew that ownership of the find had already passed to Ward's cousin, cigar manufacturer George Hull, a self-styled atheist. Hull quickly accepted an invitation to place his giant on brief display in Syracuse before hauling it to the state capital. In mid November, New York State was plastered with crudely printed broadsides inviting the curious to the Geological Hall in Albany. According to the posters, the 2,990-pound fossil was just over ten feet tall and had feet twenty-one inches long. His neck was listed as being thirty-seven inches in circumference, but his nose was only six inches in length. His right arm was said to measure just under five feet in length; it was impossible to get an accurate measurement of his left arm, since he had been lying on it.

Sculptor Erastus D. Palmer, some of whose work went into the Metropolitan Museum of Art, denounced the giant as a blatant fraud.—DICTIONARY OF AMERICAN PORTRAITS

Some of the people who saw the giant in Albany went home remarking that "after all these centuries, his face still shows that he died in agony, and his veins are so prominent in some parts of his body!"

Theories concerning the origin of the immense human were a dime a dozen. A slim majority of persons were inclined to think he had lived before or during centuries in which Native Americans made central New York their home. At least three prominent Protestant clergymen voiced negative reactions. They wanted nothing to do with the Cardiff Giant. They told anyone who would listen: "He looks to us as though he might have been carved by early Jesuit missionaries; he must have been an idol of some sort."

After the giant had been lifted from the grave in which he seemed to have lain for centuries, careful cleaning revealed new clues. On his underside, the giant's back and some of his limbs were "channeled." That is, they were deeply grooved in the fashion that running water was known to have operated on local limestone. Many visitors took these channels as indisputable

Famous showman Phineas T. Barnum made a fake copy of the fake giant and exhibited it in his New York Museum.—DICTIONARY OF AMERICAN PORTRAITS

evidence that he had been in his crude grave since close to the beginning of time.

By now, Hull had printed a brochure that he distributed free to persons who paid admission. In it, he described the state geologist as "a noted paleontologist who is among our nation's greatest scientists" and who had gone on record as saying that:

> To all appearance, the huge figure lay upon the gravel at the point where the deposition of fine silt or soil begins, upon the surface of which trees have grown for many generations. Altogether, it is the most remarkable object ever brought to light in this country, and, although probably not dating to the Stone Age, nevertheless deserves the attention of all archaeologists."

An unsigned and undated pamphlet issued about the same time, entitled *The American Goliath*, offered a brief description of the discovery of the giant plus "Opinions of Scientific Men" concerning it.

One feature of the giant that troubled some ordinary folk was the fact that he was not shaped from limestone of the region. "That's because all of his tissues were petrified," they were told by believers. Since a few voices were being raised in doubt of the authenticity of the find, a subscriber to the *Syracuse Journal* wrote an open letter scolding anyone and everyone who "is now trying to overthrow the sworn testimony of eyewitnesses and the findings of the highest scientific authorities."

A professor from Yale College went on record as believing that the giant must have gone into the ground very recently." He pointed out that it would take only a short time in the ground for all traces of marks made by tools to disappear. Since such marks were still visible, it was evident that the figure—whatever it might be—had been buried relatively recently. From New York City, famous sculptor Eratus Dow Palmer issued the most damning statement of the period. Having examined the giant from head to toe, he denounced "the figure a colossal fraud."

Such verdicts were dismissed by members of the general public, who thronged to gape at "America's greatest wonder." So many people paid admission to see the Cardiff Giant that the cigar maker who owned it took in at least thirty thousand dollars—perhaps much more.

Far too famous to remain on an out-of-the-way farm, the giant was carefully crated and shipped to New York City. To the consternation of Hull and the stunned surprise of people living outside the metropolis, there were two giants on display, not one. Located on lower Broadway, Phineas T. Barnum's Museum was exhibiting a phony giant just two blocks from where the real one was being displayed in Apollo Hall. Barnum, or one of his employees, had spent enough time with the giant from Cardiff to make surreptitious, but reasonably accurate, sketches. From these, workmen hired by Barnum crafted a copy of the figure found by Newel.

Much evidence indicates that the simultaneous appearance of two figures in New York City prompted Hull to talk—or rather, to boast. During an 1866 visit to his sister in Ackley, Iowa, Hull said, he "became enraged at the stupidity of a fundamentalist Methodist preacher." Identified only as the Rev. Mr. Turk, who was a spiritual descendant of Peter Cartwright, this Methodist preacher allegedly insisted that all who sat before him should take every word of scripture literally. This point of view, Turk reportedly demanded, applied even to a passage in the Book of Genesis that refers to an era when "there were giants on the earth."

Hull grinned broadly when describing how he and "the Reverend" engaged in a shouting match over the existence of giants in the distant past. "That incident planted an idea in my brain," he explained. "I set out to create a giant of my own in order to see whether or not folk would accept him as genuine." Newspapers that had devoted front-page stories to the Cardiff find condensed his confession and ran it on inside pages.

Mark Twain, who dearly loved a good joke at the expense of someone else, lived in Nevada briefly during the early months of the Civil War. Joseph T. Goodman of the *Virginia City Enterprise* gave him a job as a feature writer, and the native of Hannibal, Missouri, got busy. His first published hoax, which ran soon after he joined the staff of the newspaper, described a petrified man who had been found not far from Virginia City. There is no reason, however, to believe that Hull saw this piece of tongue-in-cheek journalism before himself coming up with the idea of digging up a petrified giant.

He consistently and skillfully evaded questions concerning precisely when and how he managed to produce the fake. One reporter told readers that "Hull had learned from his sister that the region around Fort Dodge holds what may be the world's largest deposit of gypsum. With this knowledge in hand, he went to the Iowa city and purchased a twelve-foot block several feet thick and secretly shipped it to a sculptor."

According to another report that may have been somewhat embellished, the man planning to create a petrified giant bought a tract of land close to Fort Dodge and hired workmen to cut an enormous chunk of gypsum from it—knowing that it was soft enough to be easily carved.

Regardless of how he got his hands on it, Hull managed to haul his huge piece of rock to the nearest railhead by wagon. From there he took it by train to a Chicago stonecutter who was

At Harvard University, interest in the strange New York find was strong enough to persuade Alexander McWhorter to pay a visit that led him to speculate that it might be of Phoenician origin.—HARVARD UNIVERSITY

willing to try his hand as a sculptor. When the "petrified giant" was completed, it was probably washed with sulfuric acid. According to later statements, Hull then persuaded the sculptor to insert darning needles into a wooden mallet and pound his work of art so that the giant would have visible pores over much of his body.

Once the work was complete, Hull shipped the sculpture to New York and smuggled it to his cousin's (Stub Newel) farm under cover of darkness. "I figured that it ought to age in the ground for a while before being dug up," he said late in life. "I really didn't have any idea how long to let it lie there, but in 1869 newspapers published a story about finding lots of fossil bones in Onondaga Valley. I waited until everybody in the region knew about the bones, then told Stub to get busy digging a new well."

Hull's accounts vary considerably in detail, and no one ever learned just how the giant came into existence. Hence the exact sequence of events that led to its unearthing is uncertain. Once the giant was found by the well diggers, however, its story became public knowledge, and it was soon after denounced as a hoax. In 1870, *Appleton's Journal* told its readers scattered

throughout the nation that Hull's find was "a clumsy forgery."
That should have ended the career of the gypsum giant, but it did
not. Numerous folk continued to consider it to be a prize they
would like to own and display. After changing hands several
times, the giant sculpture went West in 1911 when Joseph Mul-
roney of Fort Dodge purchased it. Eventually it came to adorn the
rumpus room of the Gardner Cowles, Jr., home in Des Moines.

According to scuttlebutt the New York Historical Association shelled out thirty thousand dollars in order to return the
Iowa native to the state where he was unearthed. Today the big
fellow is at the Farmers Museum of Cooperstown, New York.

In 1997, the museum's director, Gilbert Vincent, was
quoted as having said that it was about time for the giant to
go on tour, perhaps back to Iowa for a period. Maybe the big
fellow really does need to hit the road to mark his territory
and ward off the phonies. An October 1997 Associated Press
story reported that Barnum's imitation of the imitation petrified man was being exhibited in an arcade at Farmington
Hills, Michigan. There's also a replica in Fort Dodge's Fort
Museum as well as one in Circus World Museum of Baraboo,
Wisconsin.

A riddle never solved centers on perennial public fascina-
tion with a petrified giant from Fort Dodge that was long ago
recognized to be central to a huge practical joke on the American public. Why anyone will today fork over the money to
gawk at the handiwork of a cigar maker from Brighamton is a
mystery—especially since a published account says admission
is nine dollars to the tent in which the big fellow now rests.
Another piece missing from the puzzle concerns the motive of
its maker. Was he really motivated by a yearning to ridicule fundamentalist religionists, or did his encounter with a ranting
evangelist trigger an idea about a novel way to make a fast
buck?

Measured by any standard, the giant whose raw material
lay close to the Des Moines River is central to the most successful hoax of the nineteenth century. Controversy about his origin
raged so furiously that he is still given space in standard reference works.

2
Mamie Eisenhower
Army Wife

"Do you plan to follow the example of the only Iowan who preceded you here, Mrs. Eisenhower?"

"Just call me Mamie; everybody else does."

"I can't do that until we get much better acquainted, madam," responded the head of housekeeping at the White House. "I'm sure you remember that Mrs. Hoover made extensive changes and redecorated a number of rooms during her four years here. Should my staff and I be prepared to do the same for you?"

"How in the world do I know? We'll just have to wait and see. Give madam a little breathing room and let her think."

Oral tradition asserts that the wife of Dwight D. Eisenhower was furious at the suggestion that she should follow the lead of Lou Hoover. Her husband took the oath of office for the second time on Sunday, January 20, 1957, in a private White House ceremony.

Eisenhower's scruples against breaking the Sabbath persuaded him to postpone formal and public ceremonies until Monday. Ike, as he is universally known, went to the east plaza of the Capitol that day. Chief Justice Earl Warren of the U.S. Supreme Court had him repeat the oath he had taken the previous day. Returning to the White House, Ike changed out of his formal attire and told his wife: "This is it; I won't be a candidate again, so you had better make good (use) of the time we have left in this place."

Ike and Mamie had talked several times about the public's initial assumption that she would follow the example of the former

At age eighteen Mamie Doud was widely admired as "the bell of San Antonio."

First Lady from Waterloo. Therefore, Mamie said she had made up her mind to "try to please people by a piece of redecoration—maybe doing over the diplomatic reception room." It took several months to find antiques that she considered suitable for a Federal-style parlor, and when the job was completed, she informed her husband that she had "too many other things on her mind to tackle another room in this big old house." Ike noticed that she seemed a bit uncertain, perhaps even troubled, when she made that announcement. He did not pursue the matter, however, and did not have the faintest idea of what other things might be on his wife's mind.

Mamie had a great deal to think about, and she intended to think before she spoke. An old army post friend with whom she was very close at either Fort Oglethorpe, Georgia, or Camp Colt, Pennsylvania, had contacted her "out of the blue" after years of no contact. "I sympathize with you deeply about what took place in England," her friend wrote. "By now, I hope some of the wounds have begun to heal."

"Wounds? What wounds?" the mistress of the White House muttered over and over to herself. She had a few scars from old injuries, but not one of them was acquired in England. What in the world could that unexpected communication mean?

Persistent but discreet inquiry over a period of many weeks brought a totally unexpected answer to her questions. More than a decade earlier, Generals Eisenhower and Clark spent about ten days in London. There, they were assigned an Irish driver—

twenty-four-year-old Kay Summersby—who seemed to be familiar with every nook and cranny of the world's largest city. Summersby was so efficient that when Ike took up residence in London as supreme commander of Allied Expeditionary Forces, he requested, and immediately got, the young Irish woman as his personal driver. When he learned that she was engaged to be married to Col. Richard Arnold, Eisenhower flashed his famous grin and offered to dance a jig at their wedding. He never had an opportunity to act on that promise; Col. Arnold was killed in North Africa a few weeks after Ike took up residence in London.

Mamie, who could not accompany her husband, was glued to her radio on Christmas Eve 1943, when Franklin D. Roosevelt solemnly announced to the American people that Eisenhower had been chosen to lead the projected invasion of German-held Europe. Though she did not see orders sent to her husband by the chairman of the Joint Chiefs of Staff, she had been an army wife so long that she mentally paraphrased orders she knew had gone to her husband: "You will enter the continent of Europe and in conjunction with the other United Nations, undertake operations aimed at the heart of Germany and the destruction of her armed forces." Strict censorship made it impossible for Ike to confide in Mamie. Even if there had been no official restraints, he would have considered it his duty to keep silent about his plans until he was ready to act.

On May 17, 1944, he informed his immediate subordinates that Operation Overlord, code name for the Allied invasion, would be launched during the first week of June. Despite the fact that he commanded three million troops, he was keenly conscious that the undertaking could end in failure. Hence he prepared a communiqué for release in the event that his forces were turned back:

> Our landings in the Cherbourg-Havre area have failed to gain a satisfactory foothold, and I have withdrawn the troops. My decision to attack at this time and place was based on the best information available. The troops, the air and the navy did all that bravery and devotion to duty could do. If there is any blame or fault attached to the attempt, it is mine alone.

Mamie was at her husband's side at the Republican National Convention of 1952.

That statement was not made public for many months, for on D-Day—June 6, 1944—Allied forces established themselves on the beaches of Normandy. Once news of the successful invasion was made public, Mamie rejoiced at what her husband had accomplished, and she never wondered why he did not hint to her about impending movements.

Ike was away from Mamie for some time. She knew that professional soldiers are frequently required to be away from their wives for long periods and are notoriously prone to take sex wherever they can find it. She was aware that numerous females served in Allied forces and were in daily contact with males. She seemed to have been aware that Summersby, now a captain, was serving as personal secretary and military aide to her husband. But if she ever wondered what might be going on between her husband and his aide across the Atlantic Ocean, she never so much as hinted about the matter to relatives or close friends.

Ike accepted the surrender of German military forces on May 7, 1945.

To Mamie, the woman from Iowa who was beginning her second term as mistress of the White House, World War II

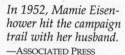

seemed almost infinitely distant in both space and time. The impending renovation of the diplomatic reception room was just around the corner. Hence a female Jeep driver seemed never to have entered the mind of the First Lady until she received that enigmatic message from a friend of long ago.

Soon after she began seeking to learn the meaning of "wounds that by now may have healed," Mamie discovered that many Americans who were stationed in London during the war believed that something was going on between Ike and his pretty aide. From long experience, she knew that rumors are likely to fly any time a group of "army grass widows" get together. Something that Ike wouldn't talk about may have taken place in London a dozen years earlier, but since gossip and truth seldom have much in common, Mamie Eisenhower dismissed the Irish woman from her mind. That course of conduct was consistent with her upbringing and early life.

Born in Boone, Iowa, on November 14, 1896, Marie Geneva Doud moved with her parents to Cedar Rapids then on to Colorado. Her father, a prosperous meat packer, tried Colorado Springs before settling down in Denver. He never attempted to explain to members of the family why he moved from one place to another, and his loved ones accepted his decisions without question.

Aside from living in Denver, Mamie—as she became known as at a young age—spent much time at her father's winter home in San Antonio. It was here that she received much of her education. It was in that Texas city that Mrs. Lulu Harris, wife of an officer stationed at Fort Sam Houston, introduced her to a second lieutenant in the Nineteenth Infantry. Dwight D. Eisenhower was instantly smitten. He explained that he was serving as officer of the day and would enjoy having her company on his rounds. She gave a vivacious nod and a smile, took his arm, and with him strolled about the army post. Within six months they were engaged to be married and were hoping that an expected promotion would come to Ike very soon. It came a few months after their marriage in February 1916 and reached him at another base to which he had been transferred.

Still a self-conscious bride, Mamie was startled when her husband came into their quarters and without a word began assembling some of his gear. She burst into tears when she realized what was taking place, then begged him not to leave her so soon after their wedding day. Ike embraced his bride before announcing: "Mamie, you're in the army now. There's one thing you just have to understand. Duty to our country comes first with me and that will never change. You come second, though."

When the pair left the White House for their retirement home in Gettysburg, Pennsylvania, Mamie confided to a cousin that she was happy at the prospect of living in a permanent home after having moved twenty-seven times with her husband and many more without him.

She remained in Gettysburg after Ike died and was visited there by Jimmy Carter during his presidency. This naturally affectionate southern gentleman kissed the widow of his predecessor upon leaving, after which she hurried to her doctor's office in order to describe the encounter. She confided: "My Lord; he surely did take me by surprise. I was so flabbergasted that I didn't know what to do. I hadn't been kissed by a man outside of the family since Ike and I said 'I do.'"

A few months before her death, the army widow watched a television program about Summersby, and as reported by friends, she "found it very amusing." At Boone, located in the Des Moines River valley, the beautifully restored Mamie Doud Eisenhower Birthplace is located at 709 Carroll Street. Though filled with memorabilia and books, it offers not a single scrap of information about Capt. Kay Summersby of the World War II Women's Army Corps. That is precisely the way Mamie would have liked her museum and library to remain.

3
Julien Dubuque

"Little Night"

Some say he did it when he wanted to make a treaty with the Fox Indians. Others say he did it when he wanted to convince the Fox to work harder for him. But whatever the circumstances, the story of his setting a river on fire is typical of those surrounding Julien Dubuque, the first white man to live in Iowa and for whom the city of Dubuque was named.

Julien Dubuque carefully crafted a reputation as a worker of magic and great wonders. He settled in a territory where the Catfish Creek flowed into the Mississippi River near the village of Kettle Chief. According to one version of the story, when Dubuque was meeting with Kettle Chief and other Fox Indians, he knew that he would need more than just words to convince them of his point of view. Before the meeting, some of Dubuque's associates went upriver and poured a barrel of oil on Catfish Creek. As Dubuque talked with Kettle Chief and the others, he was not able to get them to agree with him, so he told them that he could set the entire Mississippi River on fire. Of course, they did not believe him until he reached into a bonfire, pulled out a burning stick, and threw it on the oil slick that was just coming down Catfish Creek. The river burst into flames, terrifying the Indians. Dubuque won agreement from the Fox, and then, supposedly at his command, the fire went out as the oil slick passed. What Dubuque had done to Catfish Creek, he said he could do to the entire Mississippi River.

Julien Dubuque also said he could handle snakes without getting hurt. Once when he wanted to show his "magic" to the Fox, he picked up a poisonous snake. They watched in terror as

The old deserted shot tower in Dubuque. Molten lead was dropped from the top through small openings. The droplets splashed in a cool liquid to cool into granules.—PUBLISHED FOR NORTON NEWS AGENCY. COURTESY OF CENTER FOR DUBUQUE HISTORY, LORAS COLLEGE

the snake crawled up his arm and onto his shoulders. By handling the snake carefully and gently, he was not bitten, which added to the admiration and awe in which the Fox held him.

According to legend, Dubuque also used an eclipse to impress Kettle Chief and his people. He told Kettle Chief to have all the people assemble in one place and then reminded them of all the "magic" he had worked in the past and about how great was his power. He then promised to show them the most mighty demonstration of his power by making the sun go dark in the middle of the day. Just as the eclipse was about to start, Dubuque commanded the sun to stop shining. Of course, the sun did stop shining as the moon came between it and the earth. The Fox were astounded, and their belief in the power and magic of Dubuque was confirmed.

Julien Dubuque, the crafty worker of "magic" and "great wonders," was born in 1762 near Quebec, Canada. He grew up hearing stories of the western frontier, fur trading, and adventure.

In 1785, he set out for the West, settling for a time in Prairie du Chien, Wisconsin, on the banks of the Mississippi River. Before the French traders had arrived in Prairie du Chien, it had been an Indian village, and after the French arrived, Indians from all over the area still went there to trade with the Frenchmen. Dubuque quickly established himself as a successful trader. He was friendly, outgoing, and clever and made friends not only with other traders, but also with the Sac and Fox Indians. He wanted to learn about them and their ways, so he took time to play with the Indian children and talk with the women. He listened to the stories of hunting, of war, and of the tribes' history told by the braves. He was accepted by them as a friend, and because of his small size and dark skin, the Indians called him "Little Night."

One of the stories Dubuque heard was that a Fox woman who lived near Kettle Chief's village in what is now Iowa had discovered rich deposits of lead in the bluffs near Catfish Creek. Because the Fox sold the lead ore just as it came from the ground without being purified, they did not receive much money for it. Lead was widely used for bullets, so Dubuque became interested in the discovery, realizing that if he built a smelter, he could purify the lead ore, take it downriver to St. Louis, and get a good price for it.

Dubuque took a canoe loaded with blankets and trinkets across the Mississippi to Kettle Chief's village, and by giving gifts to a maiden named Potosa, he found the location of the lead mines.

Dubuque spent much time becoming friends with Kettle Chief and the Fox. One evening, as the braves were preparing for a ceremonial dance, Kettle Chief led Dubuque to the center of the circle near the fire. Dubuque told Kettle Chief that he did not know how to dance the ceremonial dance, but Kettle Chief had taken him to the center of the circle not to dance but to make him an honorary member of the tribe. Even with such an honor, it was no small task for Dubuque to persuade the Fox to let him manage the mines. On September 22, 1788, he signed a treaty with the Fox giving him the right to work the lead mines on the west bank of the Mississippi "as long as he shall please and (he) shall be free to search wherever he may think proper to do so."

A lead mine similar to those Julien Dubuque oversaw.—PHOTO COURTESY OF HARRY HENDERSON AND ST. JOHN MINE

Near Kettle Chief's village, "Little Night" built a cabin for himself and housing for the ten other white men from Prairie du Chien he had brought with him. They cleared the land, put up fences, and planted corn. They also erected a furnace to smelt the lead ore and mold it into bars called "pigs." Thus, Dubuque and his associates became the first white people to live permanently in Iowa.

When the French Canadians Dubuque brought with him began working the mines, they expected to employ the young, strong braves to mine the ore. Instead, they found that it was the custom of the Fox for the women and older men to do all the work. They dug the ore using picks, hoes, crowbars, or any tool they could and carried it out in baskets through tunnels that were made into the sides of the hill.

In the late 1700s, the area west of the Mississippi was under the control of the Spanish because it had been given to Spain by the French at the end of the French and Indian War. To make his claim on the lead mines doubly secure, Dubuque approached the Spanish governor-general in St. Louis, Baron de Carondele, and falsely told him that he had bought the land from the Sac and Fox, paying them in provisions, and that stakes had been set marking the land's boundaries. Dubuque also said that to honor the Spanish, he had named the mines "The Mines of Spain." Carondele gave Dubuque official title to a tract of land extending twenty-one miles along the Catfish Creek and nine miles inland. After the grant was secured, Dubuque increased his output. He built more smelting furnaces and searched for more lead ore in the hills on his land grant.

Twice a year Julien Dubuque loaded his furs and lead "pigs" on boats and went down the Mississippi River to St. Louis. Many of the Fox chiefs and braves went with him, and their arrival was always an occasion for celebration. The entourage of confident white men and colorful Fox Indians created an image of a wealthy trader from the wild frontier. The merchants, the socialites, and other leading citizens liked to see him arrive. Dubuque sold his furs and lead and purchased supplies such as powder, salt, blankets, cloth, beads, and trinkets for the Indians to last for the next six months. Banquets were given in his honor and he gave elaborate parties with plenty of food and drink. He was the center of attention because of his charm and polite manners. He played his violin and danced to his own music.

Dubuque lived among the Fox for twenty-two years. His lead mines were successful. He bought an interest in the boats that carried the ore to St. Louis, and by gaining control over the lead industry, he was able to set the price for the ore. He built an elaborate estate and lived in elegance. He should have been quite wealthy. However, he did not handle his financial affairs well and got deeply in debt to Augustin Chouteau, one of the leading merchants of St. Louis.

To settle his debts, Dubuque gave Chouteau a half interest in the lead mines and promised him that when he died, Chouteau would receive the other half. Dubuque died in 1810, but Chouteau never received the second half of the ownership in the mines. The Fox denied Chouteau's claim, stating that their agreement had been made with Dubuque only and was not transferable. Chouteau took the case to court where the matter was tied up until it finally reached the U.S. Supreme Court forty-three years later, in 1853. The Supreme Court declared that

The tomb of Julien Dubuque.—Courtesy of Center for Dubuque History, Loras College

Spanish grants were no longer legally binding, and Dubuque had not really owned the land. Chouteau was dead by then, and his heirs received nothing.

Dubuque's death was sudden. One day he developed hot skin and a pain in his chest. The Fox women tried to relieve his pain, but without success, and he died the next day of pneumonia. Kettle Chief spoke for the tribe when he said that since "Little Night" was their brother, they would bury him like a Fox. The Indian chiefs from miles around carried his body to a grave on a high bluff overlooking the junction of the Catfish Creek and the Mississippi River. They built a stone vault over the grave, covered it with lead, and erected a ten-foot-high cross with the inscription, "Julien Dubuque, Miner of the Mines of Spain; died March 24, 1810, age 45 years, six months." (He was actually forty-eight years old.)

The Sac and Fox chiefs paid annual visits to Dubuque's grave for many years, each throwing a small stone on it. Over the years the pile of stones grew quite large and covered the grave. In 1837, the city of Dubuque was built on the site of Chief Kettle's village, and in 1897 a tower was erected at the grave site reminding all who see it of Julien Dubuque, the first white man to live in Iowa.

4
Cherry Sisters
The Worst Act in Town

In 1896, when they appeared at Oscar Hammerstein's Olympia Music Hall on Broadway at Forty-Fourth Street in New York City, one theater critic said the Cherry Sisters had "the worst act ever to make an assault on the musical stage."

His evaluation was undoubtedly true. The vaudeville act was so bad that night after night for six weeks the theater was packed with people wanting to see if the Cherry Sisters— Lizzie, Addie, Effie, and Jessie—from Cedar Rapids and Marion, Iowa, would live up to (or down to) their reputation. The audiences were not disappointed. The Cherry Sisters had one of the most celebrated—and most awful—vaudeville acts of the time.

The sisters began their show with their theme song: "Cherries ripe, cherries red, Cherry Sisters still ahead; Ta-ra-ra boom-de-ay. Cherry Sisters here to stay." After a solo rendition of "Corn Juice," an Irish ballad, and a recitation, the sisters put on a skit for which they became famous called "The Gypsy's Warning" in which an evil Spanish man made romantic overtures to a lady. A Gypsy, whose daughter had died after running off with another man of whom the Gypsy did not approve, tried to warn the lady of the danger she faced.

"Lady," the Gypsy said, pointing offstage, "in that green grave yonder lies the Gypsy's only child." The warning went unheeded, the lady ran off with the evil Spaniard, and the audience guffawed—and threw cabbages, onions, turnips, and cigar butts—but no eggs. The sisters had said that if anybody threw an egg at them, they were going home to Iowa.

Addie, Jessie, and Effie Cherry, the three of the five Cherry Sisters who did most of the entertaining.
—THE *CEDAR RAPIDS GAZETTE*

Sometimes the sisters would stop a performance to criticize those who were yelling and throwing things. "You don't know anything," one sister would say to a rowdy audience. "You have not been raised well or you would not interrupt a nice, respectable show." One time Jessie got off the stage, went down in the audience, and "tapped a hoodlum on the head with a board."

For six weeks, it was great sport for New Yorkers to yell at the sisters and hurl at them "tokens of appreciation," such as rotten vegetables and fruits. The *New York Herald* even reported that "the vegetable retailers can't meet the demands of their regular customers because produce trucks and commission men are selling their vegetables directly to Hammerstein's theater patrons." It was reported that the audience would leave the theater in an "advanced state of hysteria."

Critics vied to see who could give the worst reviews. The *New York Times* said, "One short and three lank figures walked awkwardly to the center of the stage dressed in shapeless red gowns, probably made by themselves. A fat sister carried a bass drum...." Another critic commented, "Never before did New Yorkers see anything like the Cherry Sisters. It is to be hoped that nothing like them ever will be seen again." "They never missed a note," said still another critic, "or found one either."

But Oscar Hammerstein was delighted. He had been on the verge of bankruptcy due to unsuccessful acts he had booked at his Olympia Theater. When he announced the Cherry Sisters, he said "I've tried the best—now I'll try the worst." The six-week run allowed Hammerstein to pay off all his debts, although he did go bankrupt two years later.

Criticism was not new to the five Cherry Sisters. (Only four were in New York City; Ella had not gone because "someone always has to stay home to slop the hogs and milk the cow.") They were headstrong girls who grew up near Marion. After their mother died, they helped their father run his four hundred-acre farm until he died in 1885. To raise money to attend the 1893 Chicago World's Fair, the sisters formed the Cherry Concert Company and put on a show at the Daniels' Opera House in Marion. The rent on the hall was five dollars for the night and the sisters made their own crude handbills, wrote their own songs and skits, made their own costumes, and painted their hair gold with leftover sign paint. Tickets sold for ten, twenty, or thirty cents. Most agreed it was an awful show, although the *Cedar Rapids Gazette* gave the sisters one of the few reviews they ever received that was not critical:

> The entertainment given at Daniels' Opera House by the Cherry Concert Company was a polished and recherché affair. The people of this handsome overgrown village on Indian Creek, absolutely crowded and jammed, pushed and hauled, and literally walked over one another in efforts to procure seats…The public wanted fun, the public got it; the young ladies wanted money, they got it.

The sisters made $250 that night, which, they thought, was not bad for an evening's work.

Their second show, this time at Greene's Opera House in Cedar Rapids, which was one of the largest theaters between Chicago and Denver, generated the first of the reviews that told how bad the act was. The *Cedar Rapids Gazette* said,

The Cherry Sisters in their heydey.—THE CEDAR RAPIDS GAZETTE

Such unlimited gall as was exhibited last night at Greene's Opera House by the Cherry Sisters is past the understanding of ordinary mortals. If some indefinable instinct of modesty could not have warned them that they were acting the part of monkeys, it does seem like the overshoes thrown at them would have conveyed the idea in a more substantial manner....

Cigars, cigarets [sic]—everything was thrown at them, yet they stood there, awkwardly bowing their acknowledgments and singing on. Possibly the most ridiculous thing of the entire performance was an essay—think of it, an essay—read by one of the poor girls, in which she pled for the uplifting of the stage and hoped that no one would be harmed by anything they may have witnessed during the evening. The orchestra responded with 'Ra'ra'ra boom de ay.

The sisters were so offended by the review that they demanded a retraction. The *Gazette* offered to publish one, if the sisters would write it. When the paper published their long letter of misspelled words, Addie charged the City Editor, Fred P.

Davis, with libel. The *Gazette* suggested that the trial be held at
the Cherry Sisters' next performance. When the sisters
appeared on stage, the audience blew kazoos, horns, and whis-
tles. The story was picked up by newspapers all over the country, generating publicity for both the Cherry Sisters and the
Cedar Rapids Gazette.

The most famous review of the Cherry Sisters was written
in 1901 by Billy Hamilton, editor of the *Odebolt Chronicle*:

> Effie is an old jade of fifty summers. Jessie a frisky filly of
> forty, and Addie, the flower of the family, a capering mon-
> strosity of thirty-five. Their long skinny arms, equipped with
> talons at the extremities, swing mechanically, and anon franti-
> cally at the suffering audience.
>
> The mouths of their rancid features opened like caverns and
> sounds like the wailing of damned souls issued therefrom. They
> pranced around the stage...strange creatures with pained faces
> and a hideous mien. Effie is spavined. Addie is stringhalt and
> Jessie, the only one who showed her stockings, has legs with
> calves as classic in their outlines as the curves of a broomhandle.

When Hamilton's comments were reprinted in the *Des Moines
Leader*, the sisters sued the *Leader* for libel. The court ruled against
the sisters because Effie made the mistake of having the sisters put
on part of their act in the courtroom. After witnessing their performance, District Judge C. A. Bishop ruled that the ladies were
actually as bad as the review had said and dismissed the case
against the *Leader*. The Iowa Supreme Court upheld the dismissal.

In addition to their reputation for being terrible performers
and receiving bad reviews, there was the tradition of throwing
rotten fruit and vegetables and other things at the Cherry Sisters. There were reports that they performed behind a screen to
protect themselves, but they vehemently denied it. Addie once
said, "We've never played behind a screen in our lives. I believe
that we are the most misrepresented people in the United
States. Reporters can't be trusted." Such rumors, however, simply increased the popularity of the act and encouraged more
people to pay to see it. The sisters insisted that the stories of

Jessie tapped a hoodlum on the head.—THE CEDAR RAPIDS GAZETTE

rowdyism were exaggerated, but Effie herself said that in Dubuque, "We had hardly started the act when one of the ruffians in the front row turned a fire extinguisher on the stage. Instead of hitting us as intended, it struck one of the boxes." Those sitting in the box were drenched and had to leave.

In spite of the 1863 review that candidly told how bad they were and in spite of the rotten fruits and vegetables thrown at them, after their performance at Greene's Opera House the sisters went on the road. They played in Grinnell, Jefferson, and La Port City, and then toured Kansas and Illinois. Wherever they went, their show got front page notices, and people would line up for hours to see if the sisters were as bad as their reputation. Few were disappointed.

The *Iowa State Register* said, "It was the most insipid, stale, weary, tiresome two hours work we have ever seen on a stage. Everyone who laughed, jeered, hooted, or howled at them, reviled himself." After appearing in New York City, the Cherry Sisters toured California. Because they always filled the halls in which they performed, they were at one point making one thousand dollars per week, which was as much as or more than the best vaudeville performers made.

The end of the act came when Jessie died suddenly in 1903. The remaining sisters moved to Cedar Rapids, and Addie and Effie continued to perform for a few years. The sisters then opened a bakery, specializing, of course, in cherry pies.

Effie ran for mayor of Cedar Rapids in 1923 and 1925 on a platform opposing "high taxes, high skirts, high life, high utility rates." She said that public officials "waste too much time playing golf." She never received much support.

Effie and Addie made personal appearances occasionally and in 1935 revived their act briefly to appear in New York, reenacting their famous performance of "The Gypsy's Warning." They were on the same bill as Gracie Allen and Tallulah Bankhead. Their performance lived up to their reputation. It was so pathetic that, it was reported, "Gracie Allen sobbed and Tallulah Bankhead wiped her eyes."

Addie died in 1942, and Effie, the last Cherry, died in 1944. Her death was reported in a full column in the *New York Times*, telling those who had never heard the story of "one of the strangest episodes in American vaudeville," The Terrible Cherry Sisters, the worst act in show business.

Part 2
Movers and Shakers

5
Long Eye

Good Ole Boy

One by one, five railroad foremen slipped into an empty tool shed a few miles east of Fort Sanders, Wyoming. They agreed their futures were at stake when they planned their secret meeting on the last night of June 1868.

"I'm betting on Durant," one of them announced as soon as perfunctory greetings had been exchanged. "He holds the purse strings."

"But he knows little or nothing about railroad construction," an Irishman from New York protested. "He could bankrupt the project and throw us all out of work."

"I hope we won't have to take sides," another foreman interjected. "Maybe we can just keep our mouths shut, and go with the winner."

No one responded, so after a long silence he resumed his argument: "Everybody knows we're at least a year away from joining up with the Central. In that length of time, anything can happen. Durant may force Dodge out, or Dodge may make Durant put his cards on the table before showing him that he holds a royal flush." Two of his comrades nodded slowly, their body language plainly saying that three out of five were likely to favor silence and caution.

"That royal flush you're talking about could be old friends. I guess most of you fellows have heard that U. S. Grant will be here in a few days to referee the dispute?" This time, everyone nodded. Talk continued until near midnight and broke up only when all five railroaders agreed that their best course of action was to push construction ahead as fast as possible and keep

To save time and money Dodge required his men to fell trees and saw them to length, for use as crossties, without stripping them of bark.

their mouths shut. Starting work a few miles out of Omaha, it was their job to push construction of the Northern Pacific Railroad westward at top speed. Not yet operative, the line came into existence as a result of lengthy legislative jockeying.

Prominent southerners had long advocated putting federal money into a transcontinental railroad that would follow a southern route. In the 1850s, Sam Houston of Texas argued that the proposed railroad from the East to California shouldn't be built unless it crossed or came near his state. Dozens of influential but less vocal politicians from the Cotton Belt endorsed his view, and as a result none of the numerous bills introduced were supported by a majority in Congress.

The Civil War brought armed conflict between regions and simultaneously gave northerners an overwhelming majority in Congress. By 1864, a master plan had been developed and approved. From Minneapolis and St. Paul, existing railroads already ran westward. It was generally known that Abraham Lincoln put his weight behind running the railroad through Council Bluffs. According to the wartime president, there was no better tangible memorial to his presidency than completion of a transcontinental railroad.

In June 17, 1861, premature incorporation of the Central Pacific Railroad of California under president Leland Stanford and vice-president Collis Huntington had already been calculated to bring in millions of dollars. Abraham Lincoln duly signed the Pacific Railroad Act on July 1, 1862, but the nation's manpower was largely embroiled in war. Thomas C. Durant established on paper a Union Pacific corporation and framed an elaborate holding company to handle finances. Then, he poured an immense fortune into his own pockets. At the end of the war, Durant picked veteran railroader Grenville M. Dodge of Council Bluffs to bring his dream into realization.

Since the project was put on hold for the war, plans to build the railroad began almost as soon as the last shot of the Civil War was fired. Since so much distance and such formidable obstacles were involved, it was decided simultaneously to push the Central Pacific eastward from California and the Union Pacific westward from Council Bluffs. The two segments would come together at or near the border of California and Nevada. Once the rails were connected a fellow could ride on iron all the way from New York City to San Francisco.

Completion of the project required the nation's biggest expenditure ever, except for the cost of holding the Union together. Builders were lent immense sums in the form of low-interest thirty-year bonds: $16,000 per mile of track in flat regions, twice that much in difficult terrain, and $48,000 per mile of track in the mountains.

Money was the basis of disagreements between Durant and Dodge that burst into an open quarrel early in 1868. It was to the financial advantage of Durant to build as many miles of line as possible, while Dodge was determined to take the shortest practical route. He was eager to save taxpayers money, but his primary goal was to create a line along which trains could roll in the least possible time.

A native of Massachusetts, young Dodge drove a butcher's cart before studying military and civil engineering as a prelude to going West. Once across the Mississippi River, he worked briefly for the Illinois Central Railroad before becoming chief surveyor for Iowa's Mississippi & Missouri Railroad. Settling in

1869. **May 10th.** 1869.
GREAT EVENT
Rail Road from the Atlantic to the Pacific
GRAND OPENING
— OF THE —

Union Pacific

RAIL ROAD,

PLATTE VALLEY ROUTE.

PASSENGER TRAINS LEAVE

OMAHA

ON THE ARRIVAL OF TRAINS FROM THE EAST.

THROUGH TO SAN FRANCISCO
In less than Four Days, avoiding the Dangers of the Sea.!

Travelers for Pleasure, Health or Business

LUXURIOUS CARS & EATING HOUSES
ON THE UNION PACIFIC RAIL ROAD.

PULLMAN'S PALACE SLEEPING CARS
RUN WITH ALL THROUGH PASSENGER TRAINS.

GOLD, SILVER AND OTHER MINERS!

CHEYENNE for DENVER, CENTRAL CITY & SANTA FE

THROUGH TICKETS FOR SALE AT ALL PRINCIPAL RAILROAD OFFICES!

Be Sure they Road via Platte Valley or Omaha

G. P. GILMAN.   JOHN P. HART.   J. BUDD.   W. SNYDER.

An eye-catching poster invited members of the public to take part in the Golden Spike ceremony of May 10, 1869.

Council Bluffs, he surveyed much of the Iowa section of the new line, then found positions with other railroads.

An ardent patriot, the newcomer to the plains established the Council Bluffs Guard in 1856 and commanded this militia unit until the outbreak of the Civil War. When the Guard entered federal service, Dodge was made colonel of the Fourth Iowa Volunteers. Within months, he was in the thick of fighting at Pea Ridge, Arkansas, where he had three horses shot out from under him and won promotion to the rank of brigadier general.

Late in 1864, he commanded the Military Department of the Missouri for a year before resigning his commission in order to become chief engineer of the Union Pacific Railroad. His initial goal of building a mile of track every twenty-four hours was soon doubled, and then trebled. Widely known as Long Eye because of his constant use of a telescope, Dodge was considered to be the most experienced railroad builder in the nation.

That reputation, however, was not enough to shield him from clashes with Durant, whose business partners had delegated construction of the Union Pacific to him. Their simmering feud came to a public head when Durant, motivated by the fact that investors profited from every mile of track demanded that many extra miles be laid not far from the Wyoming border.

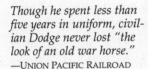

Though he spent less than five years in uniform, civilian Dodge never lost "the look of an old war horse."
—UNION PACIFIC RAILROAD

Within earshot of some of their subordinates, the ex-soldier shouted to Durant: "It's time for you to find out that men working for the Union Pacific will take orders from me, and me alone!" After having let his temper get the better of him, Dodge, it is believed, drafted and signed his resignation. He held onto it, however, when he learned that the most noted of Republicans was coming for a personal inspection of the rail line's progress.

Ulysses S. Grant, earlier nominated by his fledgling political party to run for the presidency, was considered to be a shoo-in; no political rival in the nation had anything like his personal following. Sure to win the presidential election in November 1868, Grant would have the final word concerning additional federal financing of the Union Pacific. Experts estimated that sixty million tax dollars would go into the line, along with twenty million acres of public land. To Dodge, Grant's visit meant he might have a fighting chance to thwart Durant's plans, so he kept his resignation in his pocket.

When Grant stepped from his train at Fort Sanders, he was quickly followed by two other famous fighting men—Gen. Philip Sheridan and Gen. William T. Sherman. Dodge, who could hardly believe his eyes at seeing the trio walking to meet Durant, found it impossible to conceal his elation.

Dodge first met Grant when engaged in rebuilding a Mississippi railroad; subsequently, the two men fought together in numerous battles. His ties with Sheridan were even older and closer; they became acquainted at Rolla, Missouri, in 1861. It was there that young Capt. Sheridan—"small in stature and very modest in his ways"—reported for duty under Col. Dodge. As for Sherman, he and Dodge had slept together, fought together, and rode together from Chattanooga to Savannah.

Within hours after the official train arrived, construction foremen who had wondered about their own future knew that "Moneybags" Durant had been beaten. Before Grant's showdown with Durant, Dodge told his former commander that "if Durant or anybody else changes my route, I'll quit." The future president of the United States listened briefly to Durant's arguments, then spoke loudly enough to be heard by eavesdroppers.

"The government of the United States," he snapped, "expects General Dodge to remain with the road, in full charge as its chief engineer, until the line is completed."

No doubt about it, his victory stemmed partly from his role as a "good ole boy" who hardly had to draft an argument in order to have the solid support of three men who were for many months his comrades in arms. Grant alone would have carried the day for Dodge. Backed by Sherman and Sheridan, it took the future president only a few minutes to settle the quarrel that threatened to halt the building of the Union Pacific.

When the golden spike was driven at Promontory in the Utah Territory on May 10, 1869, the Atlantic and Pacific coasts became united by ribbons of steel. Generations later, surveyors working with sophisticated new equipment managed to reduce the length of Grenville Dodge's 1,086-mile line by only 30 miles.

Upon completion of the Union Pacific, the man whom close friends described as being "obsessed with railroad building" went south as chief engineer for the Texas & Pacific. Once that

Part of the Golden Spike ceremony, as depicted by a contemporary artist.

line was in top running order, he moved on to other railroads. During half a century, Long Eye directed an estimated sixty thousand miles of surveys and supervised the building of about ten thousand miles of track. No other man has even come close to challenging that record. Although his personal fortune was estimated to have reached or surpassed twenty-five million dollars in an era when one million dollars was a sum of staggering size, he never changed his lifestyle. At his Council Bluffs funeral in January 1916, newspapers noted that he "would be forever remembered" not only as a railroad builder but also as a citizen who took an active part in the life of his city.

Had Long Eye been consulted, it is virtually certain that he would have waved aside the highly celebrated Golden Spike ceremony. His greatest victory came when three men who were vital to the Union victory in the Civil War supported his decision to lay as few miles of track as possible when completing the Union Pacific Railroad.

6
Keokuk

Mediator

Called the Watchful Fox by the white men, the Sac people called him Keokuk, which may have meant One Who Moves Warily. If that translation is correct, the title was uncannily accurate for the man who was designated by it was among the most cautious and discriminating of Native American leaders.

Born of the Fox clan in the big Sac village located on Rock Island in the Mississippi River, Keokuk is believed to have been part French. This theory was supported by the fact that he had smaller hands and feet than typical tribesmen, and his eyes were distinctly blue. About six years younger than Black Hawk, he grew up in the shadow of the older warrior.

Keokuk may have set out to compensate for his youthful appearance by developing great skill as a horseman. By the time he was initiated into manhood, he was so renowned that even the Sioux, hereditary foes of the Sac and the Fox, praised his skill and sometimes permitted him to ride with them. A very early trader described Keokuk as having "an extraordinarily resonant voice which, combined with his lofty bearing, marked him as the chieftain he was destined later to become."

When the War of 1812 broke out, Black Hawk made his way to Canada to offer his services to the British. He left behind a power vacuum that Keokuk immediately filled. Refusing to join fellow tribesmen in their assault upon Sandusky, Ohio, and other towns of the white man that lay far to the east, Keokuk was lauded by American fighting men as the "Redskin Mediator." Analysis of sparse records of the period suggest that Keokuk was motivated in part by his sincere but mistaken belief

Among the Rock River Sac, warrior Black Hawk was exalted above Keokuk but the mediator later emerged as chieftain of combined Sac and Fox tribes.

that white men would aid his people in their continuing struggle with the more powerful Sioux.

Keokuk and Black Hawk were tribal rivals during the period following the War of 1812 and before the start of the Black Hawk War twenty years later. Tradition was on the side of the warrior who led his followers from Iowa in order to plant corn in fields that were cultivated by their ancestors. Concern for the graves that dotted the countryside around their former Rock Island village was great among those who decided to fight the white man for possession of this tract. Strong emotions pulled Keokuk toward joining in this fight, but his head didn't talk to him like his heart. He and the braves who were guided by him took no part in the brief conflict; instead, they watched from the sidelines.

Pottowatamies who in 1832 killed most members of a family at Indian Creek were persuaded by Keokuk to release Rachel and Sylvia Hall for return to white settlements.

His role as an observer of both his fellow tribesmen and the white soldiers was briefly abandoned when Keokuk learned that two white women had been taken captive. He was instrumental in persuading the Winnebago to give them up. It was this episode that led some in Washington City to praise him for his cooperation with their agents on the frontier.

When the white men resoundingly defeated and captured Black Hawk at the Battle of the Bad Axe, Keokuk gained supremacy among the Sac and Fox who had settled in Iowa. Since Black Hawk was then "heavily ironed" at St. Louis, it was Keokuk who represented all Sac and Fox tribesmen when negotiating Scott's Purchase, which soon made up much of the state of Iowa. It was effected during a long parley at Fort Armstrong on Rock Island. This time, his skill as a mediator worked to the long-term benefit of his people. Since they had been defeated in war, their lands could have been taken from them in return for a few trifling concessions. Keokuk, who showed no sign of weariness after days of haggling, was eventually promised $640,000 that was to be paid in annual installments over a period of thirty-two years.

No white man appreciated the role of Keokuk better than veteran Indian fighter Andrew Jackson, who had become President of the United States. At Jackson's insistence, four hundred square miles of rich land along the lower reaches of the Iowa River were set aside for Keokuk and his followers. Under terms of the 1832 treaty, only the Iowa land designated for use by Keokuk remained in the hands of Native Americans; everything else once held by the Sac and the Fox became the possession of the United States government.

When Black Hawk was released after having been confined at St. Louis and in Virginia's Fort Monroe, he returned to Iowa as a chastened man who was remanded to the custody of his longtime rival. Keokuk, now treated as a chieftain by white men, was also designated to dispense the twenty-thousand-dollar annuity that Washington had promised.

Probably as a result of the personal interest of Andrew Jackson, in 1833, Keokuk was invited to make a lengthy eastern tour with Black Hawk in tow. Four years later, a similar itinerary was arranged for the two leaders in order to establish "for all time to come" the boundary line of Iowa. While in Washington City, Keokuk argued eloquently against some claims of the white man. Though he seems to have had little or no impact upon the final boundary line, he was lauded in *Niles' National Register* as an eloquent orator who was "one of the most sagacious Indians on our frontier."

Yet it was his defeated rival who recorded in his autobiography many details about the white man and his big villages as seen through the eyes of a warrior. Black Hawk almost certainly fused the trips of 1833 and 1837 together, but his observations have no counterpart in literature of the period. He and his companions were surprised to find so large a village when they reached Baltimore, "but the war chief told us that we would soon see *a larger one* [Philadelphia]," he said. "Our Great White Father [the president] was there, and seemed to be much liked by his white children, who flocked around him to shake him by the hand."

Passing through the City of Brotherly Love, the Sac and Fox leaders proceeded to New York. There they had one of the most memorable experiences of their long trip. Black Hawk recounts:

> We were told that a man was going up into the air in a balloon! We watched with anxiety to see if it could be true; and to our utter astonishment, saw him ascend in the air until the eye could not long perceive him. Our people were all surprised, and one of our young men asked the *Prophet* if he was going up to see the Great Spirit. The chiefs of this *big village*, being desirous that all their people should have an opportunity to see us, fitted up their great council-house for this purpose, where we saw an immense number of people.

Much to the surprise of his longtime rival and supervisor, Black Hawk had a change of heart about his former enemies. He formed a good opinion of the American "war chiefs," especially "the great war chief" [Gen. Winfield Scott]. Described by the Indian from Iowa as "a good man—one who fulfills his promises," Black Hawk looked backward and decided that had Scott been "our Great Father" in 1812, he and his followers never would have been *compelled* to join the British in their last war with America.

Having reached that conclusion, the once fierce fighting man in the custody of Keokuk continued by saying that "as our Great Father is changed every few years, his children would do well to put this great war chief in his place—as they cannot find a better chief for a Great Father anywhere." Though this pronouncement by a Native American from Iowa had no effect upon whites in the cities through which the visitors passed, in 1848, and again in 1852, Scott became a candidate for the presidency.

Keokuk never divulged his personal reaction to Black Hawk's published suggestion for solving the most vexatious of problems faced by white men. The now-venerable Sac suggested that citizens of free states having no slaves should send all Negroes within their limits to the slave states. Then all female Negroes in the slave states should be purchased by the "Great Father" and at age twelve taken to free states. This process, said the Indian leader,

During the journey to the East that was led by Keokuk, Black Hawk was sketched in the dress of a white gentleman.

would before long "clear the country of the *black skins*." Should persons in "the free states not want them all for servants," he added, "we would take the balance in our nation, to help our women make corn!" Bizarre as it sounds, the proposal framed by a Native American was about as feasible as the overseas colonization scheme favored by many whites, including the "Great Father" who was a volunteer in the Black Hawk War and was by "his children" known as Abraham Lincoln.

Soon after having led the second delegation of Sac and Fox to Washington and other cities, Keokuk began to feel cramped and confined in the four-hundred-square-mile area assigned to him. In 1845, he re-ceded to the United States the entire region and with other Sac and Fox elders moved to the region that is now Kansas. Hence, he died on Kansas soil rather than Iowa.

His name is remembered and honored by the Lee County village that became today's city of Keokuk. Located at the confluence of the Des Moines and Mississippi Rivers, it was officially named for the "Redskin Mediator" during the period in which long-simmering animosities prepared the way for the outbreak of the Black Hawk War.

7
Forest City
Hotel War

Today, Forest City is best known as the home of Winnebago Industries, builder of motor homes. However, in 1901, Forest City, a pioneer town with dirt streets, was known for having two of the finest hotels west of Chicago. The Summit and Waldorf hotels were the result of "the great hotel war" that involved almost everyone in town, cost the community thousands of dollars, and produced open hostility between people who had been friends for years. Stories of the first-class splendor and excellent cuisine of these hotels spread, and for the few months they were both open, travelers would stop in Forest City just to stay in one of the establishments.

It all started in the 1890s when Forest City's fifteen hundred people were full of civic pride. Lake Mills to the north had tried to become the Winnebago County seat in 1896, but when the citizens of Forest City raised twenty thousand dollars to pay for part of the cost of a new courthouse, the town's position as the county seat was secure. This victory developed an increased confidence in Forest City's future.

For many years, a wooden frame building had served the needs of travelers staying in Forest City, but it was hardly adequate to enhance the growing town's reputation. What was needed, said the businessmen who met at the town's Community Club, was a new hotel. The historic meeting that day included Brook Plummer, president of the First National Bank; Charlie Thompson, president of Forest City National Bank, and about fifty other businessmen.

The meeting went well. All were in agreement that a new hotel was needed as the next step in the development of Forest

The Summit Hotel was the first hotel in the city's hotel "war."—COURTESY OF VOSS MEMORIAL LIBRARY, WALDORF COLLEGE

City. Thompson suggested that the hotel be built on the north side of the city, across the street from his palatial home. Plummer, however, disagreed. He banged the table and roared, according to an account by August Lenox in the *Des Moines Sunday Register*, "Gentlemen! We're not building a farm! We're building a hotel! Put it in the business district where a hotel belongs!"

"Who's building this hotel, Brook?" shouted Thompson. "You or the businessmen?"

Plummer pulled out his checkbook. "Here's fifty thousand dollars, gentlemen, to build the hotel in the business district. If you refuse this, Thompson, I'll break you by building the finest hotel in the Middle West."

"Save that check, Brook," replied Thompson. "I am building this hotel. Beat it if you can!"

Battle lines were quickly drawn. In addition to Plummer's bank and Thompson's bank, there were two other banks in town, one of which was run by Brook's brother John. Both other banks sided with the southern site suggested by Plummer. Bank customers and others were asked to sign up for subscriptions to promote a hotel at one of the two locations. If you lived

*Brook Plummer was the
"southerner," building his
Waldorf Hotel in the business
district.*—PHOTO COURTESY OF
ARDITH HALVORSEN

in Forest City at the time, you were either a "southerner," siding
with Plummer, or a "northerner," siding with Thompson.

Thompson's group, consisting of some of the younger businessmen, bought a lot and began to build their Summit Hotel
first. Plummer moved his home and sold the lot to his group,
the Commercial Hotel Company. They began building the Waldorf Hotel a few months later. If Thompson and Plummer were
going to build hotels, they were going to be first class. Thompson was determined to build the finest hotel he could. Plummer
was equally determined to build a far better hotel than the Summit at the exact same cost—sixty-five thousand dollars—and
with materials and furnishings from the same sources.

Each hotel had about fifty rooms. They were built of the
finest Bedford brick and stone shipped from Indiana. Each was
heated by steam and had baths and electric lights. They had
elaborate card rooms, billiard parlors, reading rooms, and
dance floors, all designed by prestigious decorators brought in
from the East. More than twelve thousand dollars was spent by
each for furnishings. The hotels tried to outdo each other by

serving the finest American and French dishes created by high-paid chefs. The menus were changed daily.

Thompson's Summit Hotel opened first, in November 1900, with a spectacular gala. It was decorated throughout in lustrous black. Townspeople were carried to the hotel by the Summit's two glistening black Racine stagecoaches, trimmed in gold, and drawn by prancing jet-black horses with hand-tooled, brass-studded harnesses. When they arrived at the hotel, guests were ushered into the grand dining hall by doormen dressed in blue and gold. Waitresses in white walked across polished floors, serving the guests while music played. The luxury of the hotel was clearly out of place in this small town with mud streets and small false-front buildings.

But in February 1901, the same pageant was performed again when Plummer's Waldorf Hotel opened across the street from the courthouse in the business district. Decorated in gleaming white, everything was designed to exceed the splendor of the Summit. August Lenox described the event:

The other hotel involved in the city's "war" was the Waldorf Hotel, which still stands but now is the main building at Waldorf College. This is the dedication of Salveson Hall, October 11, 1903.
—COURTESY OF VOSS MEMORIAL LIBRARY, WALDORF COLLEGE

Charlie Thompson, the founder of the Summit Hotel in the northern part of town with his wife.—PHOTO COURTESY OF ARDITH HALVORSEN

That winter's day two teams of dock-tailed white horses pranced away from the white stone Waldorf, their heavily studded harnesses glittering in the sun. They were pulling two snow white Racine carriages trimmed in gold, and attended by drivers and footmen flaunting the dashiest in white and gold livery. What an impressive picture in white. Forest Cityans must have enjoyed that day as they were whisked through the snow for a second taste of "big town" splendor.

Forest City became famous as the "hotel town of the country." Travelers came from all around just to visit the Summit and the Waldorf. Because of the competition, a room was just one dollar per night, and for two dollars, a guest could get three French meals, a room and bath, and all the hotel's amenities.

However, the competition went beyond what might be considered reasonable. The town remained divided between advocates of the northern hotel—the Summit—and the southern hotel—the Waldorf. If a salesperson came to town wanting to do business with someone who was a "Waldorf man," he would have to stay at the Waldorf. If he also wanted to do business with a "Summit man," he would have to leave town, come back, and check into the Summit in order to call on the other person.

The animosity was so bitter that this same charade was required of farmers who came to Forest City to buy their supplies. They could not usually buy everything at one store and they too, had to check into one hotel, buy what they needed from the merchant who supported that hotel, and then leave town and return to check into the other hotel in order to buy goods from another merchant who supported the other hotel. At first, all of this was somewhat fun. But the novelty quickly wore off, and farmers took their business to other towns where they did not have to play "hotel tag."

Horse-drawn cabs from both hotels met trains as they came to town, and drivers used every trick possible to persuade arriving guests to stay at their hotel. Forest City's small boys would be on hand to watch the activity, and when a cab became stuck in the muddy streets, the boys of the opposite faction would stand around and jeer and shout. This invariably developed into fights between the two groups of boys, frequently resulting in bloody noses and black eyes.

The war could not last. Each side was losing an immense amount of money, and the battle was driving business away from Forest City. Only four months after the Waldorf opened in February 1901, Thompson and Plummer met at the Winnebago County Bank to make peace. One hotel would buy out the other. Plummer and his supporters had decided that they would offer Thompson forty-five thousand dollars for the Summit Hotel, or they would sell the Waldorf for the same amount. Thompson and his supporters bought the Waldorf and closed it.

Thompson was unsuccessful at running the Summit even without competition from the Waldorf and a Mr. Shrupp of the German Savings Bank of Dubuque, which held the mortgage on the hotel, took possession of it. However, just as the Waldorf had dwindled Plummer's fortune and the Summit cost Thompson his money, the Summit dissipated Shrupp's wealth.

In 1909, when Robert Plummer, son of Brook Plummer, offered Shrupp ten thousand dollars for the Summit, he was only too glad to sell it. The hotel continued to operate at a loss until December 20, 1915, when it caught fire and went out of existence in a blaze of glory. Today, the Forest City library stands where the grand Summit Hotel once stood, and one of the hotel's original walls is part of the library.

The Waldorf Hotel stood vacant for two years. Cobwebs and dust gathered where hilarity and splendor had reigned. In 1903, a group of churchmen under the leadership of C. S. Salveson, a Lutheran pastor, offered eighteen thousand dollars and some farmland in North Dakota for the building. Salveson remembered, "At that time, I lived in the west part of town, and every day when I walked by that empty building I used to think what a fine place that would be for a school."

In September 1903, Waldorf College, which was designed to reflect a Lutheran world view and foster an awareness of a Norwegian cultural heritage, opened. Although it was called a college, Waldorf was really an academy until 1920 when a two-year junior college program was added. In 1994, the school began to offer associate and bachelor's degrees. Today, Waldorf College is a four-year college that even has a branch campus in Tanzania in Africa.

The Forest City civil war must be one of the strangest stories to come out of northern Iowa. It was a preposterous war—intense, expensive, and over quickly. It came about when two determined bankers each wanted his own way. It divided the city. But when it was over, those who had been bitter rivals resumed friendships, and Forest City was again united in its civic pride.

8
James W. Grimes
Naysayer

A native of New Hampshire who left Dartmouth College after only three years in order to immigrate to Iowa, James Wilson Grimes settled in Burlington and soon developed a thriving legal practice. He served as city solicitor and was made secretary of a special commission named to shape treaties with the Sac and Fox Indians. His authorship of a page that ran regularly in *The Iowa Farmer and Horticulturist* helped to make his name widely familiar.

Two years after Grimes settled in Burlington, the Iowa Territory was organized and the man from the East was elected to its legislature as a member of the Whig Party. Eighteen years after coming to Iowa he became the third governor of the young state. Like Lincoln of Illinois, Grimes knew the Whig Party was losing its influence, so he followed the future president into the infant Republican Party. He did more than any other political leader to make his state "solidly Republican" and was sent to the U.S. Senate a few months before the outbreak of the Civil War.

A rock-ribbed conservative, during his tenure as governor he made some enemies because of his vetoes. One of them quashed an appropriation of five thousand dollars for a College of Physicians and Surgeons. Grimes blocked the measure because he felt strongly that men hoping to enter a profession should get their training at their own expense. Though Dartmouth College administrators disagreed with some views of their distinguished ex-student, they awarded him a Bachelor of Arts degree "as of the class of 1836."

Both Ripon, Wisconsin (ABOVE), and Crawfordsville, Iowa, claim to be the birthplace of the Republican Party in 1854.

As soon as he arrived in Washington, Grimes made it known that he would not support concessions to the "rebellious" South. This outspoken stance probably caused him to be named to a special committee responsible for the defense of the capital. Headed by Gen. Winfield Scott of the U.S. Army, the three-man body included Congressman Elihu B. Washburne of Illinois. Possibly in his official capacity as a committee member, Grimes was among civilians who made a foray into Virginia in order to watch the first major military clash between warring sections. On the field at Bull Run, he later confessed with a grimace, "I missed being captured by secessionists by exactly one minute."

Later made chairman of the Senate Committee on the District of Columbia, the man from Burlington spent so much time inspecting the city and its defenses that he missed several important speeches by colleagues. It was this factor that induced him to meet secretly with a fellow senator, probably Sen. Edmond G. Ross of Kansas, after the process that led to impeachment of Andrew Johnson was well underway.

Any novice could see that a power struggle was inevitable after the assassination of Abraham Lincoln. Lincoln had made specific plans for "reconstruction of defeated so-called seceded states," and Johnson had pledged to carry out these plans. In Congress, the group known as Radical Republicans, in which Grimes was clearly included, desperately wanted lawmakers to have charge of reconstruction so that harsh measures could be put in place.

Many members of Congress soon became furious at Johnson's stubborn resistance to what he termed "legislative usurpation of power." In a move designed to force the president to work with the aides he wished to dismiss, late in 1867 lawmakers enacted a measure forbidding him to remove key public officials without the consent of the Senate. Johnson vetoed this Tenure of Office Act, which went back to the Senate and quickly got enough votes to override the president's veto. On February 21, 1868, the man from Tennessee thumbed his nose at lawmakers and demanded the resignation of Secretary of War Edwin M. Stanton. Only three days later, 126 furious members of the House of Representatives voted to impeach Andrew Johnson for his "high crimes and misdemeanors." Only forty-seven members of the House thought he should not be impeached.

William P. Fessenden of Maine laid his political future on the line by announcing immediately that he could not support the eleven articles of impeachment that must be considered by the senators. Peter Van Winkle of West Virginia pondered for only a few days before following Fessenden's lead. John B. Henderson of Missouri and Lyman Trumbull of Illinois soon took the same stance. James W. Grimes of Iowa, Joseph S. Fowler of Tennessee, and Edmund G. Ross of Kansas were identified by newspapers as being undecided about the future of Johnson and the nation.

House manager Benjamin F. Butler, a veteran attorney with a checkered Civil War career, was chosen to fire the opening guns against the President. A correspondent for *Harper's Weekly* listened intently to Butler's four-hour speech and told readers that:

There was power in the man's coarse, big-featured face, force and aggressiveness in every line, but his curiously strange

Andrew Johnson of Tennessee, chosen by Lincoln as his running mate in 1864, wanted to carry out the "reconstruction" plans of the assassinated president.— BRADY STUDIO, LIBRARY OF CONGRESS

eyes with their half-closed lids, his hard mouth and small, drooping mustache, all combined to create an uncomfortable impression of cunning and insincerity, and his whole personality was unattractive.

To the senator from Iowa whose vote might convict or exonerate the president, Butler was much more than simply unattractive. Undocumented tradition asserts that Grimes, who listened intently during the entire time that Butler spoke in a grating voice, sometimes glanced briefly at sketches he had brought with him. If these really were the half dozen anti-Butler cartoons of legend, Grimes must have been extremely uncomfortable as he listened to the oratory of the ex-general widely known in the South as "Beast." Almost certainly having reached a decision earlier, Senator Grimes went on public record as being strongly opposed to the conviction of Johnson. Though he did not say so, his intimates knew that he had threatened to resign and return to Burlington if Benjamin F. Wade should be sent to a vacant White House as a result of a Senate vote.

Nationally renowned attorney Benjamin R. Curtis led the defense team, but it was widely acknowledged that political rather than legal issues would decide the verdict.

A young French journalist, who later became the Premier of France, was among the foreign observers who "looked in vain" at Curtis's opening speech for a strong line of defense. Georges Clemenceau strongly doubted that senators would be influenced by arguments of Johnson's attorney; he was right. More than thirty senators made up their minds that Johnson was guilty before they even heard arguments. It would take thirty-six lawmakers to convict the chief executive, however, so the

On the day of the vote on impeachment, Grimes as well as Stevens—shown here— had to be carried into the Senate chamber.—LIBRARY OF CONGRESS

issue was still in doubt when the vote was taken on May 15, 1868.

James W. Grimes, made seriously ill by high-level stress, was examined by a physician who shook his head grimly and spoke just four words to persons gathered at the senator's bedside: "He's had a stroke." Friends and admirers urged Grimes to keep to his bed at the time of the all-important vote, but he shook his head and in a feeble voice said that only death could prevent him from expressing his convictions. Said to have been carried into the Senate chamber because he was unable to walk, he knew that when he cast his vote against conviction his political career was over.

Hoping to remain in office for the rest of his term, the former governor of Iowa tried to function as a senator during the winter of 1868. Ordered by doctors to go abroad for the sake of his health, he resigned less than a year after having helped to prevent Benjamin F. Wade from becoming the nation's chief executive. In his adopted state, the legislature chose James Harlan to fill the U.S. Senate seat he vacated.

Whether or not it was Ross who met Grimes at Willard's Hotel on a night in which the future of the nation hung in the balance is unknown. Historians today generally credit the Kansan with having cast the vote by which the first impeachment move against a president was defeated. While it is true that he was the last senator to make his stance known, it is equally true that the Ross vote for acquittal might have been futile. It would have meant nothing, had not Grimes earlier committed political suicide by announcing that he would refuse to be a party to the conviction of Andrew Johnson.

Part 3
Visionaries

9

George Washington Carver

Graduate

On October 9, 1835, William P. McGinnis sold Moses Carver a slave girl named Mary. Warranted to be sound in body and mind "and a slave for life," she brought the relatively high price of seven hundred dollars. Soon after the young woman became a mother, she and her infant son were kidnapped. Carver managed to get the boy back by swapping a three-hundred-dollar horse for him but failed to recover Mary.

Nominally reared by his owner, the boy spent so much time with Mariah Watkins that he almost considered her to be his mother. He later moved into the cabin of Lucy Seymour, who warned him over and over that "a boy has got to get some learnin' if he's gonna make it in this world." It was probably at Seymour's that Carver's little boy began to call himself George Washington.

Against what seemed to be insuperable odds, George Washington Carver worked as a field hand, held tightly to every cent he earned, finally won a high school diploma, and promptly began looking for a better place to live. His "learnin'" made him itch to leave the state of his birth, in which slavery was legal, and find someplace where he could get one lung full of clean air after another, just like a white man.

Carver had earlier learned that the landmark legal case of the slave Dred Scott had been launched in St. Louis and was based in part upon his temporary residence at Fort Snelling, Minnesota. To him, that made Minnesota seem like the Promised Land of biblical fame, so with the encouragement and aid of an abolitionist physician he shook the dust of Missouri from his feet. It took only one winter for him to decide that

Iowa-educated Dr. George Washington Carver with Henry Ford.—COURTESY OF TUSKEEGEE INSTITUTE

Minnesota was entirely too cold. He heard that Kansas still had plenty of public land, so he set out for that state and found a place to settle.

Yearning for "a sure enough education," the homesteader heard rumors that there was a college in Iowa that accepted negroes. Persuaded to change states for the third time, Carver presented himself to Simpson College in Indianola where he stayed for three years working his way as a bank janitor. Proficient in both art and science, Carver chose to persue the latter.

He transferred to Iowa State College of Agriculture and Mechanic Arts (now Iowa State University of Science and Technology) in Ames in May 1891. Though barred from the college dining hall, he was welcomed into the Iowa National Guard. Despite his obstacles, Carver received a bachelor of science degree in 1894. In the following two years, he taught classes at Iowa State University while working towards his master's degree in agriculture. Booker T. Washington, who had found financial backing to launch an all-black college in the Deep South, knew that college graduates among his race were more scarce than greenbacks. Having heard of Carver, he made a trip to Iowa, was instantly impressed, and made an irresistible offer to the Simpson graduate.

It was this chain of events that took the ex-slave from Missouri to Tuskegee, Alabama, as head of the agriculture department of Washington's brand new college. Initially, Carver was largely occupied with teaching chemistry at the Tuskegee Institute, however, he soon began taking agricultural and other products to his laboratory for analysis and study. He found a way to process cotton waste so that it could be sold and developed a new strain of the sweet potato, or yam. Chemicals applied to clay from a local pit produced red, purple, and blue pigments that were suitable for use as dyes.

The agricultural chemist may have been the first educated man to foresee that one day the soybean would become a major crop throughout much of the United States. Carver's most famous work was done with the lowly peanut, however.

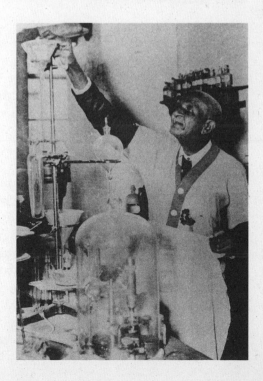

Though he was world-renowned in his later years, Carver seldom left his beloved laboratory for more than a few days at a time.—COURTESY OF TUSKEEGEE INSTITUTE

Farmers throughout Iowa and the rest of the Western world consulted Carver about crops, planting methods, and fertilizers.—COURTESY OF TUSKEEGEE INSTITUTE

Remembering from his boyhood that veterans of the Civil War bragged about having made coffee from peanuts, he made extensive tests upon the underground seeds of the plant imported from Brazil. His results surprised even the perennial optimist who made them. After becoming famous throughout the Western world, Carver had a lengthy visit with Henry Ford and reputedly told the industrial genius that he had found more than a thousand uses for peanuts. Yet when he went to the United Peanut Association meeting in Montgomery, Alabama, in 1920, the black scientist had to use the freight elevator to reach his destination.

Though urged to patent some of his important discoveries, Carver repeatedly refused, saying, "God gave these things to the earth and to me; how can I sell them to someone else?" With his eightieth birthday approaching and his health failing, the nation's most noted agricultural scientist often lifted a trembling hand in order to direct visitors' eyes to a simple framed diploma.

"If it hadn't been for a little college in Iowa," he frequently commented, "I wouldn't be here; I'd still be following a mule."

10
Theodore S. Parvin
Collector

The rarest book by Scottish poet Robert Burns, published in 1786, is entitled *The Kilmarnock*. This sought-after volume is in a niche not far from one of only two known copies of Samuel Johnson's 1755 *Dictionary of the English Language* and a table whose top was made of 37,473 pieces of wood. These unique items, along with symbolic jewels from all over the world, thousands of pieces of art in clay, bronze, bisque, and marble, and a 1540 Italian-language volume that is printed on thick black paper instead of white have one thing in common. They are all housed under the same Cedar Rapids roof.

They were brought together by New Jersey native Theodore S. Parvin, who at age twenty-one came to Iowa in July 1838. Detached from Wisconsin only one month earlier, President Martin Van Buren insisted that the new territory had to have a governor. For this office, he selected Robert Lucas of Ohio, and Lucas opted to take young Parvin along as his private secretary.

Van Buren had no idea that the official journey of these men would lead to creation of a special kind of mecca. Today, the Hawkeye State, instead of one of the great learning centers in the East, is home to the world's largest Masonic library. Iowa's claim to this library that includes numerous artifacts and antiques is the result of the unique character and dauntless persistence of the man who came to the Hawkeye State with her first governor.

At about age five, Ted Parvin suffered a fall so severe that his father and mother thought he would never fully recover. Doctors examined the boy who had become lame and decided

Parvin's dream was fulfilled in 1884 when this building was erected to house the world's largest Masonic library.

that his injury had triggered the onset of juvenile rheumatism. However bizarre their verdict may have been, their young patient walked with a decided limp for the rest of his life and because of it found himself barred from some activities in which he was keenly interested.

Two years after his injury, Ted's seafaring father gave him a special treat—a visit to the impressive local Masonic Lodge. That autumn morning set the boy's mind afire; for the rest of his life he put Freemasonry first among his many interests. After moving with his family to Cincinnati, he was disappointed when told that because of his lameness he would have to get a special dispensation to become a member of the mystical order. By all odds the most memorable day of his early manhood was March 14, 1838, when he was initiated into Nova Cesarea Harmony Lodge No. 2 in the Ohio River city.

When he reached the new western territory, Parvin found
everything entirely different from long-settled New Jersey and
the sprawling city of Cincinnati. Anytime he went walking, he
was likely to return with at least one trophy. Sometimes he had
an arrowhead, or a fragment of a polished stone axe. On other
occasions, he discovered minerals that were unusual to him.
Every time he added something to his eclectic collection, he
noted the time and place of its discovery.

Thinking of himself as an old-timer in the territory when the
third session of the legislature met in 1840, he was accosted by
another Iowan by choice. President William Henry Harrison's
untimely death after a few weeks in office had caused his aides to
scatter widely; one of them buttonholed Parvin "in the council
chamber" and requested his help in organizing a Masonic Lodge.

A dispensation came promptly, and the first Lodge in Iowa
opened at the temporary capital of Burlington on November 30.
A few months later at age twenty-four, Parvin helped to organize

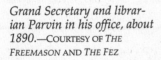

Grand Secretary and librarian Parvin in his office, about 1890.—COURTESY OF THE FREEMASON AND THE FEZ

Part of the Iowa collection as displayed at the turn of the twentieth century.
—COURTESY OF *THE FREEMASON* AND *THE FEZ*

a lodge in Bloomington (later Muscatine), where he lived at the time. Members of the order made him their Senior Deacon and then their Secretary. As a delegate to the convention that organized the Grand Lodge of Iowa in 1844, he became Grand Secretary and held the position for the rest of his life with only one brief interruption.

Though no other interest was so strong and continuous as Masonry, Parvin wore many hats. He was the principal of a public school while pursuing his studies at Cincinnati Law School. He graduated at age twenty and served as clerk of Iowa's U.S. district court for eleven years. Then, he became registrar of the state land office. Earlier, he served as the first territorial librarian and launched what is now the state library. In both Muscatine and Iowa City, he served as president of the school board. He helped to launch the Iowa State Historical Society and taught natural history for many years at what is now the University of Iowa.

Writing in 1899, Herbert S. Fairall declared that these political achievements did not match the importance of "the monument" Parvin himself erected to the glory of Masonry and of the state. That "monument," a library whose nearest counterpart in

size is located in London, was started when he had been in
Iowa only half a dozen years. At the request of the Grand Secretary, the Grand Lodge of the territory voted an appropriation
for the purchase of books.

The first appropriation was a five-dollar gold piece. Parvin
squeezed it so hard that he secured perhaps a shelf-full of pam-
phlets, magazines, and books instead of a single volume. It took
five years for the annual appropriation for books to reach
$41.50. By this time the founder of the library had enough mate-
rials on hand to warrant publication of a four-page catalog.

During its first four decades, the fast-growing institution
became home to a collection valued at twelve thousand dollars—secured one item at a time by the librarian for just twenty-
five hundred dollars.

No one ever appraised Parvin's personal library, but it was
known to be among the largest and best in the state. From it and
from his earnings he contributed liberally to the library of the
Davenport Academy of Sciences, the library that now belongs to
the state university, and the library of the state historical society.

One of his most sublime moments was the ribbon cutting of
the elegant new Masonic Library building that was opened to
the public in 1885. Complete with an alcove to hold manuscripts,

*The library's table top that
displays countless symbols
was made of exactly 100
different kinds of wood, cut
into 37,473 pieces.*

maps, and works by persons who spent all or part of their lives in the state, the Iowa Department was a source of pride and joy.

Yet the Grand Secretary/Librarian also reveled in the General Museum with its exhibits and a clipping bureau that was one of the first of its kind in the nation. Located at 813 First Avenue S.E. in Cedar Rapids, Parvin's "monument," which is now a magnet for scholars, is open to the public free of charge.

Iowa gets short shrift in "Points of Interest" described in the AAA *North Central Tour Book*. Though the section is only thirty-two pages long, its editors take care to see that the library launched with five dollars by an avid collector is represented in the most widely used of all travel guides.

For information about the library and its hours call (319) 365-1438.

11

Brigham Young

Way Station

Thomas L. Kane, an adherent of the religious organization that by 1850 was almost universally known as the Mormons, reached Iowa during the spring. He considered settling in Zarahemla, the short-lived community established by and for members of his faith, but learned that if it still existed, it was about to go under. As a result, he headed for the western border of the territory.

Before arriving at Council Bluffs, Kane knew that it was a point of departure for a twelve-hundred-mile trek through "Indian country." He expected to find a number of fellow believers at this jumping-off place. Astonished at what he saw there, he described it in detail:

> This landing and the large flat, or bottom, on the east side of the river were crowded with covered carts and wagons; and each one of the Council Bluff hills opposite was crowned with its own great camp gay with bright white canvas and alive with the busy stir of swarming occupants.
>
> In the clear blue morning air the smoke streamed up from more than a thousand cooking fires. Countless roads and by-paths checkered all manner of geometric figures on the hillsides. Herd boys were dozing upon the slopes; sheep, horses, cows, and oxen, were feeding around them and other herds in the luxuriant meadow of the then swollen river. From a single point I counted four thousand head of cattle in view at one time.
>
> As I approached the camps, it seemed to me the children there were to prove still more numerous. Along a little creek I had to cross were women in greater number than the

blanchisseuses [professional wash women] upon the Seine
[River] washing and rinsing all manner of white muslins,
red flannels, and parti-colored calicoes and hanging them to
bleach upon a greater area of grass and bushes than that of
Washington Square.

There was something joyous for me in my free rambles
about this vast body of pilgrims; I could range the wild countryside wherever I listed!

At age fifteen, Vermont native Joseph Smith began to have
visions. Seven years after these experiences started, he said that
an angel delivered to him a set of golden plates covered with
strange characters. Smith, who vowed that he had supernatural
aid in the task, translated and published the lengthy material
received in so strange a manner. When *The Book of Mormon* came
from printing presses at Palmyra, New York, in 1830, a powerful new religious movement was launched.

With a handful of followers, Smith moved to Ohio and Missouri before establishing an Illinois headquarters. When Smith
was killed by a lynch mob in 1844, Brigham Young assumed the
mantle of leadership. Though Young approved the printing and
brief use of special currency at the Illinois center called Nauvoo,
he was convinced that Mormons would have to go to a remote
place in order to find peace.

His fears were well founded as local residents held meetings concerning these "invading religious zealots." Informal
"conventions of citizens" had met at both Quincy and
Carthage, Illinois, in order to sponsor resolutions that
demanded removal from their state of "every one of these vile
polygamists who call themselves Mormons." The editor of the
Quincy Whig informed his readers that "it will be in vain for
them [the Mormons] to contend against the public sentiment;
all must go."

After conferring with his Council of Twelve, Young
responded to demands for removal with a promise that his followers would shake the dust of Illinois from their feet "as soon
as grass grows and water runs." That meant there would be no
spring planting at Nauvoo the following year.

Joseph Smith was led by visions that begin in 1820 to become founder of the Mormon Church.
—COURTESY OF CHURCH OF JESUS CHRIST, LATTER DAY SAINTS

Despite the pledge that Illinois would soon be free of Mormons, many of those who hated them most were not satisfied. Gov. Thomas Ford, whose four-year term of office was about to expire, warned that the "spirit of the people is up, and signs are very evident that an attempt will be made from the surrounding counties to drive the Mormons out."

In this explosive climate, Ford asked political leader Stephen A. Douglas to urge Young to accept an accelerated timetable. A handful of Mormons decided that they were strong enough to show nonbelievers they meant business, so they crossed the frozen Mississippi River as soon as its ice was hard. This token migration ended at Sugar Creek, Iowa.

Young came across a report by explorer John Charles Frémont that he considered to be a miraculous sign. After reading and digesting it, he concluded that the Great Salt Valley in the faraway Utah Territory would be an ideal haven. Hence, one of the biggest mass migrations in U.S. history got under way early in the spring of 1846. Any family still in Illinois after April faced a threat of being burned out by vigilantes. A correspondent for the

St. Louis Daily Republican rode to Nauvoo to take a first-hand look at the largest city in Illinois. He found that "the city and country present a very altered appearance," and told readers that:

> There are no crops, either growing or being planted. In many instances, the fences are down and houses have been deserted. The whole aspect of the country is one of extreme desolation and desertion. At nearly every dwelling, where the owners have not sold out and gone, they are making preparations to leave. Nearly every workshop in the city has been converted into a wagon maker's shop.

Several long-established trails linked the heavily populated East with the untamed West, but by going through Iowa the migrants could shorten their journey by many miles. Young's decision to take a shortcut may have been influenced by one of the most colorful frontiersmen of the period. Isaac Galland, who called himself Doctor, had earlier secured titles to large tracts of land on both sides of the Mississippi River. Ostensibly he was interested in helping the Mormons; however, Galland hoped in

In October 1838, citizens of Missouri launched a program of systematic terror, killing Mormons wherever they could be overpowered.

When Joseph Smith was killed by a mob in 1844, Brigham Young stepped into the leadership vacuum that had been created.

vain that many or most of them would buy land and become permanent settlers on homesteads secured from him.

The Mormons crossed the Mississippi River at or near the mouth of the Des Moines River. Their caravans meandered slowly west by northwest. Affluent Mormons rode in covered wagons, but great numbers of them walked. It was a major undertaking to get across even a small stream, so progress was slow. At Mosquito Creek and other spots, migrants sometimes camped for weeks. Their journey of nearly 150 miles across the newly organized Iowa Territory ended at Council Bluffs, where they established the semipermanent camp that Kane found to be mind-boggling in size.

After Iowa was admitted into the Union, the base that many Mormons called Winter Quarters was slowly shifted to the west bank of the Missouri River. Today, Interstate 80 crosses the state in a relatively straight latitudinal line before veering southward to Council Bluffs.

Brigham Young and his close advisors led an estimated sixteen thousand followers across what is now the state of Iowa. He tried to maintain military discipline while on the march, and often succeeded. Groups of Mormons, usually less than one hundred in number, traveled in the charge of a leader they called their centurion. It was this officer who each morning signaled for the bugle call to be sounded; he also decided how much time could be devoted to activities such as dressing, eating, and praying.

Some centurions permitted families and individuals for whom they were responsible to spend a week at especially fertile spots in order to plow and then to plant corn. Members of later caravans, it was believed, could pause a day or two in order to harvest these crops. Though this sporadic effort seems to have fed a few hundred persons briefly, most were bone-tired and famished by the time they reached the Council Bluffs encampment. During their first winter at this encampment, an estimated eight hundred Mormons died of cold, disease, and hunger.

The departure of Brigham Young and his immediate followers for faraway Utah did not end the Mormon presence in Iowa. Young, who had briefly served as a missionary in England, sent teams of Mormons to the island kingdom. They found it easy to recruit converts from among the great masses who were jobless as a result of the industrial revolution.

Hundreds, then thousands, of new converts crossed the Atlantic Ocean in steerage. Many of them chose New Orleans as a point of departure for "the land of milk and honey" that they had been assured was waiting for them. They traveled up the river to Keokuk by steamer where they then headed toward the far West.

When the railroad reached Iowa City in 1855, that became the end of the line. Many British Mormons flocked to New York, where they took trains for Iowa City by way of Chicago. At the point where the rails stopped, great numbers of Mormons embarked upon what may have been the strangest of all American migrations. Accompanied by a few ox-drawn supply wagons, contingents of travelers left Iowa City pushing specially made hand carts. The pace of oxen limited their progress to about two miles a day. Despite their slow pace, only a few hundred died en route to Utah. Viewed in retrospect, this

In 1846, an amateur artist depicted the big Mormon camp at Mosquito Creek, Iowa.
—COURTESY OF CHURCH OF JESUS CHRIST, LATTER DAY SAINTS

migration out of Iowa was one of the most remarkable achievements of the century.

If Galland had been more persuasive in extolling the virtues of what really was the most fertile land on the continent, would the great Mormon Temple be sitting today in Iowa City or Des Moines or Council Bluffs? Not a chance. Young was so obsessed with his dream of utopian life in a region he had never seen that to him, the land of tall corn was only a means to an end.

12
Amana Colonies
The Promised Land

The dream of a perfect community—one without crime, without poverty, without persecution; one in which all live together in true brotherhood, usually sharing all things—was frequently attempted in nineteenth century America. Most such communities were based on religious beliefs and were set apart from neighboring towns. These communities usually were not able to sustain viability and faded away after a few years. Iowa's Pella, which was founded in the 1840s by Dutch immigrants led by Dominie Sholte, and Tennessee's Rugby, which was founded by British author Thomas Hughes in the 1880s, are two such communities that have been able to maintain their original identity.

The Amana Colonies was unusual among utopian communities because it was a successful communal society for eighty years and then transformed itself into a capitalistic society while retaining its religious heritage. It lasted longer as a communal society than any other such group in America except for the Shakers.

The Amana Colonies had roots in nineteenth century Germany where Christian Metz, a carpenter, declared that he was a prophet and that God spoke his will through him. A group called True Inspirationists accepted Metz's leadership. Because the True Inspirationists were at odds with the established church, they were persecuted by both political and religious officials.

In the midst of this persecution, Metz said that God revealed to him that the True Inspirationists should move west, and so he and three others traveled to America, where in 1842 they bought five thousand acres near Buffalo, New York. They

Early life at the Amana Colonies.—COURTESY OF AMANA COLONIES CONVENTION AND
VISITORS BUREAU

sent word back to Germany that the Promised Land had been
found, and by 1843 eight hundred members of the Community
of True Inspiration had arrived to build five villages in western
New York called the Ebenezer Society.

One of the principles the community developed was that
everything would be owned in common, based on the Bible's
observation about the early church that "all the believers were
together and had everything in common. Selling their possessions and goods, they gave to anyone as he had need." (Acts
2:44-45 NIV). This was not one of the original principles of the
community, and it took several years for it to become accepted
by everyone in the society.

During the years the True Inspirationists were in New York,
they worked out this and other practices necessary for living
together successfully. Their lives centered on their faith and the
communal system of living allowed members to give more
attention to their calling of serving the Lord. Everyone contributed his own skills, and the community was able to establish
woolen mills, saw mills, flour mills, and other industries and
became prosperous. The people were solemn and sober and

believed that they should remove themselves from the influences of the world. They spoke only German and did not allow idle talk. Both men and women dressed in muted colors, usually black. They lived in plain homes decorated only with vines and colorful flowers.

As Buffalo grew, it expanded toward Ebenezer and various temptations were placed before the members of the community by their worldly neighbors. In addition, the True Inspirationists were threatened and disturbed by those from the nearby Seneca Indian Reservation. Metz and the elders agreed that to maintain their way of life and dedication to God, they needed to move where they would be more isolated from the rest of the world. They sent a delegation to explore possibilities in Kansas but found nothing to suit them. In 1855, however, they purchased twenty-six thousand acres in the fertile Iowa River valley twenty miles west of Iowa City, which was the state capital at the time.

The True Inspirationists dismantled their mills and factories in New York, transported them west, and rebuilt them in six vil-

A woman weaving a basket, one of many occupations offered at the Amana Colonies.—Courtesy of Amana Colonies Convention and Visitors Bureau

lages near the Iowa River. Since the railroad ended at Iowa City, everything they brought from Buffalo had to be carried by ox cart from Iowa City. Amana—which means "believe faithfully"—was the first village to be laid out in 1855. Over the next ten years, five more villages were established: West Amana, South Amana, High Amana, East Amana, and Middle Amana. In 1861, the Mississippi and Missouri Railroad was continued west of Iowa City through a village called Homestead. The Amana elders decided they needed a town on the rail line to send their products to the outside world, so in 1865, they purchased Homestead, which became the seventh Amana colony.

Each of the seven colonies had farm buildings, factories, between forty and one hundred homes, a school, a post office, a wine cellar, a general store, a meeting house, and a kitchen house. Although each family lived in its own home, food was prepared in the kitchen house where as many as fifty people could eat together in a large dining room. Some people, however, would take food from the kitchen house back to their home to eat, a practice that was uncommon at first, but contributed to a change in the nature of the Amana society as it became practiced more and more.

Life in the seven Amana Colonies was communal. Each person contributed his or her labor according to the direction of the elders of the church, which oversaw the community. Children went to school until they were fourteen, at which point they were given jobs that they kept for the rest of their lives. Typically boys were given the same craft as their fathers and girls would work in the kitchen house. In certain instances, the elders chose someone to go outside the colonies to receive specialized training as a doctor, a dentist, a teacher, or other professional. The society paid for this training and the individual knew that as soon as the education was finished he was to return to the Amanas.

All things were provided to community members—housing, food, clothing, medical care, education. Children were taught to read and write in German and church services were in German. The Society took care of every need and emergency. Women with children two years old or younger did no

Woodworking is another important occupation at the Amana Colonies.
—COURTESY OF AMANA COLONIES CONVENTION AND VISITORS BUREAU

community work. Older members were respected and cared for. Courtship was done under the guidance of the elders. If two people wanted to get married, they had to have a year's probation during which time they were to live in different villages. At the end of the probation, if they had remained faithful to each other and their spiritual zeal was undimmed, they were permitted to marry.

The center of community life was the church, which usually met eleven times a week. Men and women entered the church building through different doors and remained separate throughout the meeting, with the elders sitting at the end of the room facing the congregation.

For eighty years—until the 1930s and the Great Depression—the Amana Colonies prospered as one of the most successful examples of communal living in the United States. There was full employment and a high standard of living because of the efficiency and quality of the people's work. There was peace and prosperity. The church was in charge of the community's businesses and government as well as its religious affairs.

The Amana Colonies was successful in part because it achieved a balance between the demands of communal living and the individual's desire for personal possessions. In the homes, men, women, and children all had their own rooms, which they could furnish as they wished.

But the people of the Amana Colonies were not isolated from the changes brought by the twentieth century. More and more families chose to eat in their individual homes instead of the dining rooms in the kitchen houses. An agricultural depression of the 1920s affected Amana as much as it did their neighbors. But it was the automobile that had the greatest effect on Amana. Visitors from the "outside" began to come to the colonies, and the young people of Amana were able to take jobs in Cedar Rapids and Iowa City. Then World War I brought fear of anything German or communistic. This led to a suspicion of people who lived in the Amana Colonies because anyone using the German language was suspected of being a spy, and any hint of communal sharing was regarded as un-American. The Great Depression of the 1930s brought even more pressure to the community and led the elders to study what changes should be made.

In June 1932, the society voted to become capitalistic. It became a corporation and all members received shares of stock depending on their length of service to the society. They bought their houses or built new ones. The corporation continued to make and sell fine furniture and woolen goods, and it has developed a tourist industry with restaurants and tourist attractions. The name *Amana* is probably best known today as a home appliance manufacturer, a company the society established in 1937 and later sold to an outside corporation.

The seven Amana Colonies have continued to prosper under their capitalistic structure as much as they did under a communal way of life. The faith has been kept and is still practiced, but the old way of life has been lost forever. What remains in the Amana Colonies is a museum of the past that has become one of Iowa's leading tourist attractions.

13
Carrie Chapman Catt
Strategist

"Make some noise if you must—but *keep it impersonal; never, never attack a member of the legislature by name.* When you dress for the march down Broadway, remember that your goal is winning political support—not attracting attention. Do not for a single instant forget that you are a foreigner here—Tennessee and the other states of the Deep South resent our presence, and we must act accordingly. Does anyone have any questions?"

Briefing her troops for a public assault upon long-established customs, Carrie Chapman Catt was hopeful but cautious. She made an inflexible rule to avoid predictions of victory. Nashville, Tennessee, was crucial to the adoption of the Nineteenth Amendment to the U.S. Constitution. After studying several cities, Nashville was selected for the campaign, but in the event of a failure the fallback list could be analyzed once more.

In today's climate, few local or national elections entice half of the registered voters of a given city or state to go to the polls. It is difficult to envision the political landscape of the 1920s in regard to the Nineteenth Amendment. Many precinct or ward bosses used a spittoon to express their opinions of "female agitators who want to change things." If such a fellow did not make it clear by his words, his actions shouted loudly enough. By spitting his tobacco juice into an enamel container, he said that he would like to spit on the "whole gaggle of crusading women."

Viewed from the perspective of the twenty-first century, it seems all but unbelievable that Abraham Lincoln became president of the United States in 1860 by winning the votes of one out of every eighteen Americans. Suffrage was narrowly limited

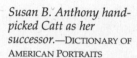
Susan B. Anthony hand-picked Catt as her successor.—DICTIONARY OF AMERICAN PORTRAITS

in the era just prior to the Civil War. In most states, the only persons eligible to vote were white males, age twenty-one or over, who owned property or could show proof of military service.

Union victories on battlefields, rivers, and seas brought an end to slavery, and the Fourteenth Amendment conferred citizenship upon ex-slaves. Orator Frederick Douglass, supported by numerous ardent abolitionists of the northeast, thundered that citizenship was not enough. Black males, he insisted, were as entitled to vote as were their white counterparts. Resistance to his proposal was not limited to secessionist states; throughout the North there was widespread opposition to any move that would permit ex-slaves or black freedmen to have a part in choosing officials.

In this climate of agitation, a handful of determined women converged upon Washington and held the first National Woman's Suffrage Convention. Local and state conventions had met earlier, and at Akron, Ohio, delegates heard the most "moving" presentation on the subject ever to come from "human lips." It was delivered by Sojourner Truth, who had been born as a slave named Isabella. A formal resolution passed in January 1869 by the Washington convention warned that "*a man's* government is worse than *a white man's* government, because, in proportion as

New York publisher Frank Leslie left his fortune to his wife, having no idea that a sizable portion of it would help to fund the crusade for woman suffrage.—DICTIONARY OF AMERICAN PORTRAITS

you increase the tyrants, you make the condition of the disenfranchised class more hopeless and degraded." This challenge fell largely upon deaf ears. Five weeks after adjournment of the convention, Congress enacted the Fifteenth Amendment aimed at granting suffrage to black males and sent it to the states for their vote. Partly because it was viewed as a punitive measure aimed at the rebellious South, ratification came relatively easily. Even though black males were allowed to go to the polls, often in order to help send a member of their race to a high political office, black and white females were barred from participation.

Under the leadership of Susan B. Anthony, the women's movement remained alive, but it progressed at a snail's pace. Only after the western territories became states did females begin to vote at the local level. When she moved to Iowa from Wisconsin at age seven, no one anticipated that little Carrie Lane would become a chief strategist of the national drive for equality of the sexes at the polls.

Carrie's farmer father didn't think a girl should try to get a college education. However, determined to study at what is

Catt frequently invoked the memory of Frederick Douglass, who was almost as interested in suffrage for women as for males of his own race.

now Iowa State University, Carrie taught for a year, and she "squeezed every penny until it hollered to be turned loose." Her nest egg, along with part-time work while a student, kept her in college without a break until she graduated in 1880—first in her class.

Carrie read law but soon decided that she would rather be principal of the high school in Mason City than become a practicing attorney. Less than two years later, she was in charge of the entire school system. At age twenty-four, she succumbed to the blandishments of newspaper publisher Leo Chapman and reluctantly gave up her career to become his wife. Subscribers probably didn't know it at the time, but young Mrs. Chapman helped edit and manage the *Mason City Republican* until she became a widow at age twenty-seven.

On her own, the Iowa State graduate worked in California for a year as a reporter before returning to Iowa, where she soon became active in the state's suffrage association. When she went to the East in 1890 in order to participate in the National American Woman Suffrage Association (NAWSA), she discovered that western women had much greater freedom than those on the other side of the Mississippi River.

Having known George Catt at Iowa State, she did not discourage the attentions of the wealthy engineer and eventually agreed to marry him—under certain conditions. Days before the ceremony, George signed a document and had it notarized. Predating today's prenuptial agreements by many decades, this contract stipulated that Mrs. Catt would be free of all other responsibilities for four months a year so that she could work for the suffrage movement. Immediately after the marriage ceremony she startled old friends by announcing that she would drop her birth surname in favor of her given name and the surnames of both of her husbands, thus becoming Carrie Chapman Catt.

Susan B. Anthony was greatly impressed by the woman from Iowa at their first meeting and soon decided that when she retired she would pass the mantle of leadership to her. That is how a woman almost unknown nationally became president of the NAWSA in 1900. She served only four years before giving up the office in order to be with her dying husband. When George made her a widow for the second time, he left her enough money to make her financially independent for life. Once she was again free to travel, she went to Europe to help found the International Woman Suffrage Alliance and to preside over its biannual meetings.

Called back to the presidency of the NAWSA in 1915, she found the organization penniless and in shambles. Her first move was to retreat to a spot where she would not be disturbed in order to draft a detailed six-year "Winning Plan" with an overtly political goal. The widow of publisher Frank Leslie, who made a fortune from his famous illustrated newspaper, gave Catt two million dollars with which to set her strategy into motion. Carefully guarded as a secret until victory was in sight, it was her plan that led President Woodrow Wilson to laud her as "a strategist with few equals." From Paris in May 1919, the president sent a long cable that helped to push the Nineteenth Amendment through Congress.

Congressional approval of the measure that was designed to put women on an equal footing with men at election time

Carrie Chapman Catt "rested from her labors" by writing a book, Women Suffrage and Politics *(1923).*—NATIONAL ARCHIVES

was one thing; ratification by thirty-six states was an entirely different matter. Catt's detailed plan brought thirty-five ratifications without a great struggle, but all remaining states were known to be stubbornly opposed to letting women vote. Her decision to try for the final ratification in Tennessee took her and her followers to Nashville, where every idea proposed was submitted to her and approved before it was implemented.

Before the governor was persuaded to call a special session of the legislature in order to consider the amendment, it was widely known that the measure would have strong support in the Senate. When it passed by a 25 to 4 margin on August 13, 1920, Catt warned her lieutenants that "the real fight is still to be won," for the House was evenly divided. Every time it seemed a vote in the lower chamber was imminent, someone managed to win a postponement.

During insufferably torrid summer days it seemed that the liquor interests, political machines, clergymen, and big business would defeat the crusading women. Catt picked the brains of veteran Tennessee legislature watchers and smiled grimly upon finding that the youngest member of the house was the son of one of her staunch supporters.

Tradition has it that emissaries of the Iowa educator managed to spend an entire evening with the mother of Harry Burn on the eve of the all-important vote. Whether that was the case or not, the representative of a grimly conservative district voted in the affirmative on August 18, and the long fight was over. Eight days later U.S. Secretary of State Bainbridge Colby certified passage of the Nineteenth Amendment and announced that millions of American women were eligible to vote in November.

Catt issued a statement in which she reminded the nation at large that:

> Women of this country have for fifty-two years been engaged in a campaign without a pause. It was a continuous, seemingly endless chain of activity. Young suffragists who helped to forge the last links of the chain were not born when work on it began. Old suffragists who forged the first links were dead long before it was finished.

She said nothing about having devoted nearly all of the thirty years since she left Mason City to the crusade. Instead she devoted her time and energy to devising a strategy to keep the feminist movement alive. Her efforts made the National League of Women Voters her lasting legacy. Carrie Chapman Catt would hold her head high if she knew that her brainchild is a political force so potent that every seeker of national office courts its support.

Part 4
Record Makers

14
Herbert Hoover
Fall Guy

On November 7, 1928, a banner headline in the late edition of *The New York Times* heralded Herbert Hoover's triumph in the presidential election and pointed out that Democrat Alfred Smith lost his native New York. The paper noted that the decades-old Democratic hold on "the solid South" was broken—largely because many in the region couldn't persuade themselves to vote for a Catholic.

Florida, Kentucky, Tennessee, and Virginia were listed in Hoover's column, and in six other Cotton Belt states the outcome of the election was still considered to be doubtful. A final tabulation showed Hoover with forty states and 444 electoral votes, while New York Governor Smith took only eight states and 87 electoral votes.

Had Jesse Clark and Huldah Minthorn Hoover been alive, their joy would have been unbounded. Both of them had died, however, half a century earlier at about age thirty-five. Jesse went first during the last month of 1880; Bert was just six years old when he attended his father's funeral. To make things easier for widows, relatives often kept their children for months or years; Huldah's second son lived briefly in an uncle's sod house in Sioux County. He spent most of the rest of that year with another uncle who was superintendent of the Osage reservation at Pawhushka in the Oklahoma Territory.

About two years after his father's death, Bert's mother followed her husband to the grave, and the three Hoover orphans were divided among relatives. Bert was taken by farmer Allan Hoover, so he lived for a time on a West Branch farm. One year later, Uncle John Minthorn, a Quaker frontier physician living at Newberg, Oregon, lost his only son. He found consolation of a sort by informally adopting Bert and moving to Salem.

His subsistence-level boyhood plus his many changes of residence prevented the Hawkeye State youth from winning a high school diploma. Still, he was eager to go to college. To encourage him, "Pappa John," as he called his benefactor, suggested that he apply to a brand new institution—Leland Stanford Junior University at Palo Alto, California. Bert failed the entrance exam but won conditional admittance after taking a college preparatory course. In October 1891, he attended his first class at age seventeen and four years later became the youngest graduate of Stanford.

While at Stanford, he met the love of his life, Lou Henry. Though both later insisted that they did not experience "love at first sight," Lou and Bert saw one another regularly during the remainder of his senior year. By the time he walked across the platform to accept his diploma, they had arrived at what they described as "an understanding." That is, they were seriously interested in marriage but had no plans to marry until Lou graduated.

Influenced during adolescence by engineer Robert Brown, young Hoover decided to become a mining engineer. Specializing in geology, he worked for survey teams for three summers but failed to find a job as a surveyor when he graduated. Ready and willing to work at any available job, Hoover signed up to push ore carts at the Reward gold mine near Nevada City, California. He later said he pushed a cart in the lower levels of the mine for fifty cents an hour.

Lured to San Francisco by job opportunities, Bert worked briefly as an office clerk before landing a position as a mining engineer with Bewick, Moreing, and Company. His first professional job required him to go to Coolgardie, Australia, where he was put in charge of inspecting properties the London-based company was considering for purchase.

Scouts for other mining enterprises had examined the sprawling Gwalia fields and had recommended against purchasing them. Hoover spent weeks at the place, became enthusiastic

Floor of the stock exchange during the panic, as seen by a New York World *artist.*

about it, and persuaded executives in London to take the plunge. Land plus equipment cost them an estimated five hundred thousand dollars—but the field discovered by the twenty-four year old from Iowa produced one million dollars or more in gold annually for many years.

While Bert was in Australia, Lou was finishing up her senior year. As graduation time approached, he sent her a one-sentence cable from Down Under. She promptly responded to his proposal from halfway around the world with a simple "Of course." Bert sent his resignation to London, wrapped up his work, made arrangements to start a new job, and returned to California for a simple marriage ceremony early in 1899.

Hoover's work in Australia had drawn the attention of the Chinese Bureau of Mines, and the engineer, now married, went prospecting in the Chihli and Jehol provinces. Lou was a lover of languages and took this opportunity to learn some Chinese.

Bert didn't find any gold worth mining, but he did find immense deposits of high-grade coal. After her husband stumbled upon the coal, which the Chinese were unaware of, he spent longer and longer periods in the field. That gave Lou the freedom to devote many days to her study of language. Before she had been in Tientsin a year, she had mastered the rudiments of both spoken and written Chinese.

Her new skills proved invaluable in the wake of an uprising known in the West as the Boxer Rebellion. Finding it impossible to topple the empress dowager T'zu Hi, members of the Society of Boxers turned their wrath against foreigners in Tientsin. When the city came under siege, Lou Hoover was the only person who knew English, Latin, French, Chinese, and a bit of German. Serving as interpreter, she played a significant role in preventing the massacre of non-Chinese residents during a three-week siege of the city.

After leaving China, Hoover organized his own engineering firm and offered to explore natural resources anywhere in the world. He may have been the first westerner to conclude that Russia held immense oil reserves, but the government of the czar did not encourage his efforts. Turning his attention to Burma, he sank everything he had into a silver field at Bawdwin.

When Lou's husband (center) opened the baseball season at Griffith Stadium in Washington, the nation was rosily optimistic.

He hit pay dirt almost immediately, and before he celebrated his thirtieth birthday, the mining engineer from the states was worth at least four million dollars.

Hopeful that the "progressive wing" of the Republican Party would become dominant, in 1912 he made what was then considered to be a stunning political contribution—one thousand dollars to Theodore Roosevelt's third-party try for the presidency. Roosevelt's Bull Moose party won six states, but their combined electoral votes were just one-fifth of those garnered by Woodrow Wilson. His big political contribution brought him to the attention of Washington however, and Hoover was picked by President Wilson to head a series of relief efforts in Europe. He then became U.S. Food Administrator after the nation entered World War I.

Hoover's support of Warren G. Harding in 1920 brought him a cabinet post, which he retained during the Coolidge administration. As secretary of commerce, Hoover was constantly the subject of newspaper headlines for expanding the Bureau of Standards, seeking to regulate the "newfangled" radio, boosting commercial aviation, sparring with agriculture secretary Henry C. Wallace, and leading the nation's first concerted effort to reduce unemployment. Hoover headed a commission that recommended the building of the St. Lawrence Seaway and argued eloquently for the construction of Boulder Dam.

Calvin Coolidge stunned his party and the nation in 1927 with a single sentence: "I do not choose to run in 1928." With the field wide open, Hoover's reputation plus his optimism about banishing poverty took him to the White House in March 1929.

Within weeks, the mining engineer accustomed to analyzing statistical reports saw that the prosperity he envisioned was threatened by a number of factors. Farm prices were slipping because production was exceeding demand. U.S. industries were finding it difficult to participate in world trade because the nation's high tariffs angered leaders of other nations. Corporate profits were spiraling upward at a cost to consumers—wages were kept low, and consumer purchasing power was limited. It would take time to effect change in all of these areas, and a fourth major factor identified early on by the new president was

At age twenty-four, Hoover was photographed in Australia.

beyond his influence. Easy credit plus loose record systems encouraged speculation, especially in securities that could be bought on a 25 percent margin.

By September 1929, Hoover publicly expressed concern that the production of iron and steel was dropping. Almost as soon as this trend was identified, he learned that British interest rates were due to rise to 6.5 percent—a move sure to cause investors in the island kingdom and in Europe to liquidate vast holdings of U.S. securities. Still, neither the chief executive nor Wall Street analysts anticipated what was to come.

On October 24, the economy showed signs of a loss of confidence as the stock market began to take a plunge on what became known as Black Thursday. On October 25, more than twelve million shares were dumped by investors. Before the gloomy day ended, five prominent Wall Street bankers met in the offices of J. P. Morgan & Co. After a brief conference, they released a statement saying that the fundamentals of the market were sound, and that the bad day had been caused by technical

Lou Hoover was the only First Lady who mastered the Chinese language—both spoken and written.

factors. A late order for two hundred thousand shares of steel left the financial world reeling but optimistic. Four days later, a headline in the conservative *New York Times* summarized events of the day that became known throughout the world as Black Tuesday. The Dow Jones Industrial average plummeted almost thirty-one points and thousands of investors hurried to dump securities they had bought on margin. In a single business day, an estimated thirty billion dollars in capital simply evaporated, setting the stage for the onset of the Great Depression.

Within months, the prosperity promised by Hoover turned into adversity. Average weekly wages dropped to twenty-eight dollars, and the income of nearly three-fourths of all American families dropped below the twenty-five hundred dollars per year that was considered essential for a decent standard of living. Blue-chip stocks rallied early in 1930, then took another steep plunge. Rolls of the unemployed jumped to four million.

At the University of Pennsylvania, Simon Kuznets launched an economics statistics study that culminated in formulating the

Gross National Product (GNP) index. During a special session of Congress, tariffs were raised to their highest level in the twentieth century despite the fact that more than one thousand leading economists signed a petition opposing this move. Other industrial nations promptly raised their tariffs in retaliation, and world trade was stifled.

During Hoover's third year in the White House, conditions went from bad to worse. An estimated twenty thousand business establishments declared bankruptcy and more than sixteen hundred banks went under. Average weekly wages dropped to seventeen dollars and the GNP fell to a trifle over half of its 1929 level. From a high of 381 on September 3, 1929, the Dow Jones average fell to 41.22—its lowest point ever. By December 31, nearly seventeen million unemployed workers swelled bread lines and twice that many had no income from any source. Automobile sales, which topped five million in 1919, dropped below one million. A crowd of three thousand demonstrators at a Ford plant in Detroit drew fire from police that killed four people and wounded nearly one hundred. Charged with having participated in a riot, the wounded were taken to hospitals where they were handcuffed to their beds.

Our nation's thirty-first president agonized over these and many other tribulations, but he hit an emotional bottom when twenty-five hundred impoverished veterans of World War I descended upon Washington in May. Since the movement started on the West Coast, its members adopted the slogan, "Coming for Justice—Eastward Ho!" Many of those who walked as far as two thousand miles were accompanied by hungry and ragged wives and children who hoped their presence would persuade lawmakers to advance the date on which they would be paid. Most of them hoped to get about five hundred dollars in "bonus payment" for service overseas.

Appeals to the chief executive proved futile; Hoover refused to see their leaders. Angry publishers of the *Bonus Expeditionary News* portrayed the man from Iowa in a steel hat like that worn by German soldiers in World War I. Reporter Drew Pearson of the *New York Sun* inspected the improvised shacks in which veterans camped in Anacostia Flats near the Capitol and grimly wrote that he could see "no hope in their faces."

Troops were ordered, probably by the president, to disperse the marchers. Led by U.S. Army Chief of Staff Douglas MacArthur, cavalry and infantry units used tanks and gas grenades to drive veterans from their makeshift quarters. MacArthur was assisted by Maj. Dwight D. Eisenhower and Maj. George Patton.

Whether they had the wealth of Andrew Mellon or were forced to abandon the Bonus Expeditionary March, all Americans took it for granted that the sitting president would be nominated for a second term. Inevitably, Hoover became the Republican candidate when the first ballot was taken in Chicago in June 1932. Ten days later, Democrats, who also met in the stadium, nominated Franklin D. Roosevelt of New York as their party's candidate.

When voters went to the polls on November 8, Hoover's native state went to his rival. Hoover carried only Connecticut, Delaware, Maine, Vermont, Pennsylvania, and Nevada to win fifty-nine electoral votes against Roosevelt's forty-two states and 472 electoral votes. Though he did not become bitter, the native of West Branch, Iowa, realized that he had been made the fall guy for the Great Depression.

Hoover holds an all-time record as the chief executive whose administration was most battered by economic developments over which he had no control. Today, the most tangible memorial to the Iowa orphan sits astride the Colorado River in Black Canyon. Boulder Dam was completed in 1936 when the last of 4,400,000 cubic yards of concrete were poured. Eleven years later, the "political fall guy of the Great Depression" received a vindication of sorts when Boulder Dam was renamed Hoover Dam. On August 10, 1962, the Herbert Hoover Presidential Library and Museum was dedicated in the town of his birth, West Branch, Iowa.

15
Cap Anson

3,041 Hits

Though his family had lived in New York's Duchess County for five generations, Henry Anson struck out for what he considered to be the West as soon as he was grown.

In southern Michigan, he stopped roaming and married a local girl, but by 1851, he realized he was nowhere near the real West. He set out without having chosen a destination, located a good plot of ground near the Iowa River, and with the help of friends, built a log cabin. By the time it was finished, he decided to make it a town, so he called it Marshall—later Marshalltown since Iowa already had a Marshall.

On April 17, 1852, Henry's wife presented him with a brawny little son who cried so loudly that neighbors claimed they heard him from half a mile away. Remembering good times in small towns of Michigan, the boy's father named him Adrian Constantine for two of his former haunts. That strange name may have had at least a minor role in shaping young Anson's early character.

"I was a natural-born kicker," he admitted years later, "a hell-raiser bent on making trouble for others. I was born with strong dislike for two things—work and study—and I shirked both of them at every chance I got."

More than anything else, the boy whose name became abbreviated to Cap every time he served as captain of a sports team—which was mighty often—liked to play ball. Along with his father and older brother, he learned how to handle a ball skillfully by spending entire afternoons playing "bull pen," which offered American men as well as boys a chance to get off

Anson was still youth-fully slender when he first played for Chicago.

the farm or out of the mines. A variation of this game, "one o' cat, two o' cat," called for a careful eye at the plate and fast running when a hit was made.

Baseball, considerably more structured than these games after being codified a few years earlier, reached Marshalltown when Cap was thirteen years old. Within months, his father had helped organize the Marshalltown Baseball Club. Along with his two sons, Henry played every chance he got. Sometimes the town nine, financially backed by the successful hotel that Cap's father operated, went as far afield as Omaha to meet and usually trounce rival teams.

Henry Anson stuck his thumbs into his vest and held his head high any time someone bragged about his younger son's skill as a ballplayer, but he desperately wanted the boy "to make something of himself."

Packed off to the University of Iowa, Cap was thrown out for misbehavior and sent to Notre Dame for a period. After having been twice dismissed from college, Anson came back home to Marshalltown while still in his teens. He divided most of his days between baseball and billiards.

By that time, a handful of teams had "gone professional." One of them, the Forest City Club from Rockford, Illinois, came to Marshalltown in 1870 to play the local yokels. Their pitcher, Al Spaulding, saw Cap in action and persuaded his coach to give him a shot at the big time during the following year by playing for Rockford at sixty-five dollars a month. Almost before he became accustomed to wearing a uniform, Anson learned that his club had joined nine others to form the National Association of Professional Base Ball Players. This arrangement took the boy from Iowa, who admitted to teammates that he still had corn tassels stuck behind both ears, to Boston, New York, Chicago, and Philadelphia.

By 1895, Cap (center) was beginning to develop the paunch that was later a prominent physical feature.

In the City of Brotherly Love, the gangling young fellow from the Hawkeye State nearly dropped his teeth when the Athletics offered him $1,250 to play with them in 1872. He grabbed the unexpected opportunity and spent the next five years with the team. Though he never pitched during this period, he played every other position—and off the diamond gambled in billiard halls, punched policemen in the nose, and fell in love with Virginia Fiegal who said she would marry him if he would quit drinking. Cap watched with interest from a distance as men with money bargained over putting together a National League. Shortly after it was formed, Cap went to William Hulbert's Chicago White Stockings.

After giving up baseball, the record-maker from Iowa toured for five years as an actor.

By 1879, the Iowan who developed skill on sand lots had been a catcher, first baseman, outfielder, shortstop, third baseman, and second baseman. To the club's owner, that rounded experience plus his growing reputation as a batter was enough to make him both manager and team captain. In that dual role, Cap decided he would hold down first base for a while but didn't anticipate that he would stay there for nineteen years.

In his role as manager, some sportswriters believed that lung power was his greatest asset. Writing in the *New York Times* in 1922, one such person said that, "In his impassioned moments, Anson had a voice like a hundred Bulls of Bashan." His never-to-be-forgotten roar stemmed partly from the fact that he was several inches taller and fifty or sixty pounds heavier than the average big league player of his era. Denying that size had anything to do with his lung power, Cap told yarns about his boyhood during which he spent "hour after hour at the edge of a field of corn yelling until every stalk was bent toward the distant horizon."

He was better than good at every position he played, including first base, but it was his prowess with the bat that put his name in the record books. During the 1883 season, he scored six runs in a single game. Beginning the following year, for six consecutive seasons he drove in a hundred or more runs per season. In 1897, when he was forty-five years old, Cap chalked up his three thousandth hit. Four years later, during his final season as a player, his record stood at 3,041 hits in spite of the fact that for more than twenty years his team played little more than a hundred games annually.

Communication and travel was a lot slower then. Yet the slugger from Iowa was known and lauded throughout the nation—partly because he was a superb showman as well as record-maker. When the Republican National Convention came to Chicago in 1888, every member of Cap's team was wearing a black swallow-tailed coat when he marched onto the diamond. His natural ability as a headline-grabber paid off again the next season. His players lost fewer games than any other team up to that time. Cap refused to answer questions during the season, but at its triumphant end he bragged to reporters that he "took his men to Sulphur Dell for three weeks of spring training and all that sulphur water really paid off." Three years later, tired of sometimes being derided as "elderly," he donned a false beard just before a game started.

Vachel Lindsay, who preceded Carl Sandburg as poet laureate of the Windy City, wrote that Anson was Chicago's "darling pet and pride." Any photo or engraving that included him was a prized souvenir, and "Anson bats" were sold at ball parks and sports stores everywhere.

After Cap gave up baseball, he spent a lot of time in billiard parlors and on golf courses. His name is sprinkled across pages of record books, but in order to find it you'll have to look for Adrian C. Anson rather than Cap or Pop as he was widely known in his years as manager.

Whatever name he was called by, the burly fellow from Marshalltown was the champion batter of the National League in 1879, 1881, 1887, and 1888. He's listed as champion manager of the National League five times—1880, 1881, and 1882 along with a double comeback in 1885 and 1886. After the National Baseball Hall of Fame was established at Cooperstown, New York, Adrian Constantine Anson was inducted in 1939—just three years behind George Herman ("Babe") Ruth.

16
Meredith Willson
The Music Man

Meredith Willson was still a teenager when he moved from Mason City to New York. Although he never lived in Iowa again, he is strongly identified with the state, and his incredibly popular 1957 Broadway musical *The Music Man* glorified turn-of-the-century Iowa. He has been known as "Iowa's best friend" and wrote what became the official song for the state's hundredth birthday celebration in 1946:

IOWA, it's a beautiful name
When you say it like we say it back home,
It's the robin in the willows,
It's the postmaster's friendly hello.
IOWA, it's a beautiful name
You'll remember it wherever you roam;
It's the sumac in September,
It's the squeak of your shoes in the snow.
It's Sunday school and the old river bend,
Songs on the porch after dark;
It's the corner store and a penny to spend,
You and your girl in the park.
IOWA, it's a beautiful name
When you say it like we say it back home,
It's a promise of tomorrow
And a memory of long ago.
IOWA, what a beautiful name
When you say it like we say it back home.

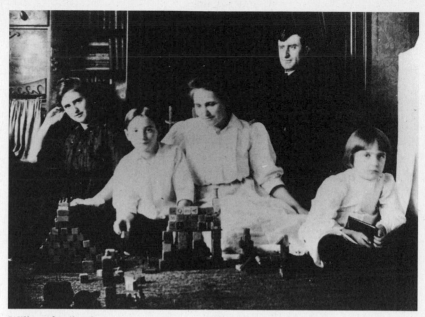

Willson family photo.—MASON PUBLIC LIBRARY HISTORICAL COLLECTION

Meredith Willson was the third child born to John and Rosalie Willson. John was a banker and a lawyer; Rosalie operated the first kindergarten in Mason City, gave piano lessons, and was Sunday school superintendent at the Congregational Church.

John and Rosalie believed they could shape an unborn child's destiny by what they did during pregnancy, and their experience seemed to verify the theory. They wanted their first child to be a writer, so they spent nine months talking about famous authors and all things literary. They put pictures of famous writers around the house.

Their first child, Dixie, did become a writer of children's stories, radio shows, and screenplays. Once she was an elephant rider in the Ringling Brothers Circus for more than a year while she did research for one of her books that has been called, "The best book ever written on the circus." John and Rosalie wanted their second child to be a business executive and Cedric became vice president of Texas Industries. John and Rosalie focused on music during the third pregnancy, and—perhaps as a result—

Meredith became one of America's most popular musicians and composers.

Meredith Willson was born in 1902 in Mason City. He weighed fourteen pounds, seven ounces, and was the largest baby born in Iowa up to that time. When the baby was one week old, he had still not been named, so the names Alonzo, Buford, Meredith, Rex, and Roderick were written on five pieces of paper and put into a hat. Dixie, who was then twelve years old, drew from the hat the piece of paper with *Meredith* on it. And that was how he got his name.

Meredith's was a musical childhood. He learned to play the banjo, piano, mandolin, guitar, and ukulele. One of his childhood friends said that Meredith's mother told Dixie, Cedric, and Meredith that they could own and play as many musical instruments as they wanted. Their house was alive with music. Rosalie Willson encouraged her children to believe they had the power to do anything they wanted to do.

One day, Meredith's piano teacher, who was also the band director, talked Meredith's mother into letting him learn to play the flute. She saved money from her piano lessons and ordered one from a Chicago mail order catalog. When the silver flute

Cedric, Meredith, and Rosalie Willson at the piano.
—MASON CITY PUBLIC LIBRARY HISTORICAL COLLECTION

Meredith Willson singing You and I, *which hit the charts in 1941.*—Photo by Safford Lock, Aug. 1941, Mason City Public Library Historical Collection

arrived, Meredith did not know what to make of it. He thought it looked like a soft drink bottle and couldn't figure out where to blow it. He wanted to send the flute back, but his cousin convinced him it would be too much trouble to return it. Meredith and his piano teacher together studied from an instruction book and eventually, he did learn to play it. He learned to play the piccolo as well.

When he was eleven years old, Meredith and his brother, Cedric, who played bassoon, joined the "Boys Band" organized by a man named J. H. Jeffers, one of the people Meredith remembered when he created Harold Hill in *The Music Man*. In high school music became the focus of Meredith's interests. "Music is all I care about," he said. Between freshman and sophomore years of high school, he played flute for eight weeks with an orchestra at the Lake Okoboji resort. He played banjo in the high school orchestra. He wrote a song for his senior class. All the while, Meredith's ambition was to play flute and piccolo in the famous John Philip Sousa band.

When Meredith moved to New York City after high school, his career skyrocketed. He went to New York in 1919 to study flute at the Damrosch Conservatory (now the Julliard School of Music). A year earlier, his sister, Dixie, had moved to New York where she worked as a dancer in the Ziegfeld Follies and as a critic for Fox Film Company.

In 1920, Meredith received such a strong recommendation that he was able to join the flute-piccolo section of the John Philip Sousa Band without auditioning. He traveled widely in the U.S., Canada, and Cuba with the band. He particularly enjoyed playing the famous piccolo solo in Sousa's "Stars and Stripes Forever." Every season with the band closed in Madison Square Garden with a spectacular concert by four hundred musicians including sixteen piccolos, forty trumpets, thirty trombones, and twenty drums.

In 1924, Willson left the Sousa band to join the New York Philharmonic as the first chair flutist under Arturo Toscanini. When he was only twenty-four years old, Willson conducted the American Philharmonic, becoming the youngest philharmonic master in America.

In 1929, Meredith and his wife, Peggy, a childhood sweetheart, moved to San Francisco where he became musical director of KFRC radio. The 1930s were spent working in radio and motion pictures. During this time he composed about four hundred musical numbers including *The San Francisco Symphony* in honor of the completion of the Golden Gate Bridge in 1937 and *Missions of California*. In 1940, he wrote the musical score for *The Great Dictator*, Charlie Chaplin's first talking picture.

Serving as head of the Armed Forces Radio Services during World War II, working as musical director for the *Burns and Allen Show*, writing "May the Good Lord Bless and Keep You"—which sold more than five hundred thousand copies in four months—for NBC's *The Big Show* all made Meredith Willson an important and well-known musical figure in America.

However, he is best known for writing the lyrics and music to the Broadway hit musical *The Music Man*. He began writing it in 1952, and rewrote it nearly forty times before its Broadway opening on December 19, 1957, at the Majestic Theatre. Willson composed fifty musical numbers for the show but only thirty were used. *The Music Man* was an instant success and made

Meredith Willson leading the marching band at the Band Festival for the press premiere of Music Man.—PHOTO BY ELWIN MUSSER, JUNE 1962, MASON CITY PUBLIC LIBRARY HISTORICAL COLLECTION

Meredith Willson famous. It won the New York Drama Critic's Award for Best Musical, Best Music, and Best Lyrics. It won five Tony Awards and was named Best Musical by both *Variety* and *Sign* magazines.

The story of *The Music Man* takes place in River City, Iowa, in 1912. River City is Mason City as Willson remembers it being when he was ten years old. Professor Harold Hill, the music man, is a traveling salesman who comes to River City to organize a band. He wants to sell musical instruments and band uniforms and then leave before anyone figures out that he cannot read a note. He convinces the parents of River City that their children can be saved from the bad influence of the town's pool hall by buying his musical instruments. The only problem is that he gets caught up in the life of River City and falls in love. *The Music Man* is full of memorable tunes such as "Seventy-Six Trombones," "Marian the Librarian," and "'Til There Was You." Willson once commented, "I didn't have to make up anything for *The Music Man*. All I had to do was remember!"

Willson went on to write other musicals such as *The Unsinkable Molly Brown*, about an Irish woman who came to America to seek her fortune; *Here's Love*, the Broadway version of *The Miracle on 34th Street* that included the song "It's Beginning to Look a Lot Like Christmas;" and *1491*, a play about what happened before Columbus discovered America. He is one of the few playwrights to have had three plays on Broadway at the same time.

In the years that followed, Meredith Willson received many awards, including two honorary doctorates. President John F. Kennedy cited him as The Nation's Big Brother of the Year, the Salvation Army recognized him for his contributions to American music and human betterment, and he was a candidate for the *Guinness Book of Records* for conducting the largest marching band with more than three thousand musicians. In 1963, the movie version of *The Music Man* premiered in Mason City to great fanfare.

Meredith and Peggy, his first wife, were divorced in 1948. She felt his work commanded too much of his attention. He then married Ralina Zarova, a Russian opera singer who had been in the United States for one year. They were constant companions until Rini died of cancer in 1966. He later married Rosemary Sullivan, a secretary in the Paramount Studios Music Department.

Meredith Willson died in June 1984 and was buried in Mason City, Iowa. Since his death, the Mason City Foundation has restored his boyhood home as a tourist attraction and in 1999, began building a ten million dollar Music Man Square that will include the Meredith Willson Museum and Music Conservatory, a multipurpose Reunion Hall, and the Meredith Willson Theater.

At the time of Willson's death, Robert Stone, pastor of the Congregational Church in Mason City, said, "Meredith lived his life as a walking, talking, singing, and dancing salesman for Mason City and Iowa." As he said in *The Music Man*, "You really ought to give Iowa—Hawkeye Iowa, Dubuque, Des Moines, Davenport, Marshalltown, Mason City, Keokuk, Ames, Clear Lake—ought to give Iowa a try."

17

First Events and Achievements

353 Years

1640—French trappers first record their observations of Sioux Indians who are hereditary foes of tribes in Iowa.

1673—Jacques Marquette, Louis Jolliet, and seven companions become the first Europeans to see Iowa from the river on which they are traveling.

1788—Julien Dubuque becomes the region's first white settler and soon makes the first great treaty with American Indians of the region, acquiring about 140,000 acres.

1796—Spain makes the first of many mineral grants in the region that will become Iowa; Julien Dubuque is given title to "The Mines of Spain."

1804—Explorers Lewis and Clark spend their first day in Iowa on July 18.

1805—Under Thomas Jefferson, the Territory of Louisiana— including present-day Iowa—is formally established.

1805—Lt. Zebulon Pike selects what he considers to be a favorable site, and the work of building the first fort—Fort Madison—begins.

1812—Black Hawk's first significant military expedition consists of an attack upon Fort Madison, which was destroyed and abandoned within months.

1813—William Clark, who earlier explored part of Iowa with Meriwether Lewis, becomes the first governor of the Territory of Missouri—which includes Iowa.

1830—Iowa's first school is opened near Montrose by teacher Berryman Jennings, in a log cabin provided by Isaac Galland.

Iowan by choice Amelia Bloomer was the first person in the state to have her surname enter everyday speech as the name of a garment.

1834—Iowa becomes part of the Territory of Michigan.

1836—Iowa becomes part of the Territory of Wisconson.

1838—Government of the Territory of Iowa is launched at Burlington on July 4.

1839—Iowa City becomes the capital—it was moved from Burlington.

1842—Methodists establish Iowa Wesleyan as the state's first college.

1842—Black Hawk, who launched the conflict that bears his name, becomes the first American to deny that private persons are entitled to own land.

1844—A convention meeting at Iowa City adopts the first constitution of the State of Iowa; a great seal is soon designed and put into use.

1845—A Masonic Library, destined to become largest in the world, is founded at Cedar Rapids by the Grand Lodge of Iowa, A. F., & A. M.

1846—Three days after Christmas, with the year about to end, Iowa is admitted into the Union.

1846—Grinnell College is the first four-year liberal arts college west of the Mississippi River.

1848—The newfangled telegraph is used in Iowa for the first time.

1853—Antoine le Claire breaks ground for "Iowa's greatest venture"—the Mississippi and Missouri Railroad, destined to become the Chicago, Rock Island, and Pacific.

1855—A. C. Dodge becomes the first U.S. Senator whose father is also a member of the body; Pappa Henry was elected from Wisconsin.

1856—For the first time, a locomotive appropriately known as "the Des Moines" crosses the Mississippi River using a bridge started two years earlier in order to link Rock Island with Des Moines.

1856—The beginning of the year sees the state's first railroad go into operation, stretching all the way from Davenport to Iowa City.

1857—Des Moines becomes the capital of Iowa.

1860—The State University of Iowa is chartered, and Silas Totten accepts the presidency.

Launched with an appropriation of five dollars, the Masonic Library in Cedar Rapids is now the largest of its kind in the world.

1861—At Wilson's Creek, Missouri, Shelby Norman of Company A, First Iowa Infantry, became the first Iowan to die in the Civil War.

1862—Francis Jay Herron, age twenty-five, becomes the youngest Civil War major general at this time.

1865—Abraham Lincoln selects Council Bluffs as the eastern terminus of the nation's first transcontinental railroad.

1865—The state's tobacco crop exceeds three-quarters of a million pounds for the first time.

1866—Secretary of the Interior James Harlan authorizes the first controversial payment of annuities to Mesquakie Indians living in Iowa.

1866—After having conducted the state's first geological survey, C. A. White announces that, in his opinion, the likelihood of finding oil is very slim.

1869—Arabella Mansfield graduates from Iowa Wesleyan and soon becomes the first female attorney in the nation.

1869—On August 7, E. C. Pickering makes the first photo of a total solar eclipse.

1869—Iowa Agricultural College, chartered in 1857, opens at Ames.

1871—Though carousels had been around for a spell, no one bothered to seek a patent until it is granted to a Davenport resident on July 2.

1873—The world's largest cereal factory (Quaker Oats) is established in Cedar Rapids.

1874—Born in West Branch, Herbert Hoover becomes the first president born west of the Mississippi River and the first millionaire president.

1877—The long-anticipated canal around the Des Moines Rapids at Keokuk, built at a cost of $4,500,000, accepts its first traffic.

1877—This is the first year in which both old settlers and newcomers can use the telephone in the state—if they can afford it.

1883—Herbert Hoover, the first future president to become an orphan, loses his mother three years after the death of his father.

1883—In Mason City, feminist leader Carrie Chapman Catt becomes the first female superintendent of the trans-Mississippi city's schools.

1885—With the year just four days old, the first appendectomy is performed at Davenport.

1890—At Muscatine, triumphant innovators produce the nation's first buttons fashioned from freshwater pearls.

1892—With the flow of mail from Iowa increasing by leaps and bounds, J. S. Duncan invents the addressograph at Sioux City.

1892—At Independence, John Johnson becomes the first bicyclist to ride a mile in less than two minutes from the starting line.

1894—The USS *Ericsson* is launched at Dubuque and is hailed as the first warship built on inland waters.

1895—"Uncle" Henry Wallace establishes the *Wallace's Farmer*.

1896—They didn't dream it would have such an impact, but

Well ahead of her followers, one of the chief strategists of the women's movement led a sedate parade down Pennsylvania Avenue.

in Iowa City the first intercollegiate basketball games featuring five-man teams are played on January 16.

1899—Lou Henry marries Herbert Hoover, not dreaming that the ceremony will lead to her being the first First Lady to be born west of the Mississippi River.

1902—In Charles City, Charles H. Parr and Charles H. Hart establish the first successful tractor company.

Herbert Hoover, the first self-made millionaire to become President of the United States, was the first chief executive born west of the Mississippi River.

1902—The first statute that makes school attendance compulsory instead of optional goes into effect.

1905—The first concrete cantilever bridge in the United States is opened at Marion.

1906—Shortly before or after this year, the first unit of what is now the International 4-H movement is organized in Clarinda.

1907—The word *tractor* is coined.

1915—The national horseshoe pitchers' association holds its first tournament at Kellerton.

1917—The nation's first U.S. Army training camp for black officers opens for business on June 15, with persons who complete the course of training headed "Over There."

1918—Carrie Chapman Catt becomes the first Iowa woman to be lauded after having been consulted by a U.S. President—Woodrow Wilson.

1920—Near Cedar Rapids, Mrs. Jens G. Thuesen becomes the first woman to vote in a national election.

1922—At Onawa the Eskimo Pie is patented by C. K. Nelson and soon has nationwide popularity.

1924—The first national corn husking championship, held at Alleman, sets contestants and spectators into a frenzy of sneezing.

1929—Iowa export John Wayne becomes the first actor destined for greatness who insists upon performing his own stunts.

1932—The first organized dumping of milk is staged as a protest against low prices; earlier, Herbert Hoover brought Theodore Roosevelt to the state as mediator.

1934—For reasons not fully explained, Oskaloosa becomes the first U.S. city to fingerprint all of its citizens.

1937—At Cedar Rapids, the first commercially made trampoline is an instant success.

1952—Raging waters of the Missouri and Mississippi Rivers cause the greatest flood damage in the history of the state up to this time.

1959—The first plane crash in which most members of a famous musical group are killed takes place soon after takeoff from Clear Lake. Buddy Holly, Ritchie Valens, and J. P. "Big Bopper" Richardson have just performed in the Serf Ballroom and are headed to Moorhead, Minnesota, for another concert when their plane goes down, killing all aboard.

1967—Amana Radarange becomes the first home microwave oven.

1970—At Davenport, C. A. Browne becomes the first black contestant in the Miss America pageant.

1972—The first time the national presidental caucuses begin in Iowa.

1993—Worst flood in Iowa's history leaves Des Moines without water for thirteen days in July.

18
The Wallaces

Good Farming, Clear Thinking, Right Living

Henry A. Wallace, the only U.S. vice president from Iowa, was more than just a political figure. He probably had a greater influence on agriculture in Iowa—and the rest of the United States—than any other person. He was an idealist and reformer who predicted that one day all Americans would live in affluence, and he worked toward fulfilling that prediction. Wallace was a scientist, a journalist, U.S. secretary of agriculture, and vice president.

As a scientist, he was one of the pioneers in the development of hybrid corn. "It was the development of hybrid corn," said Joseph Frazier Wall in the book, *Iowa, A Bicentennial History*, "that had the greatest impact upon the Iowa farmer in the twentieth century and has enabled the state to become a granary for the nation and the world." As a journalist, he made *Wallaces' Farmer* into the most influential farm journal in the nation. Through *Wallaces' Farmer* he championed the cause of farmers even though it meant fighting against the establishment. Wallace believed the free market operated to the disadvantage of the farmer because the more of a commodity that was produced, the less the market would pay for it, and because the market was not quite free but was manipulated in favor of the buyers.

As secretary of agriculture and vice president, "Henry A. Wallace was one of the most colorful and controversial personalities to emerge out of the New Deal," said Edward L. and

Frederick H. Schapsmeier. "He often sounded like some latter-day prairie prophet summoning a lost generation to the Promised Land." As part of the Roosevelt administration, Wallace was the architect and administrator of massive programs that improved the way of life for American farmers. It was only as a politician that Wallace's success was not evident. After serving as vice president under Roosevelt, he ran for president in 1948 as the Progressive Party candidate. That candidacy tarnished his image because of the Party's association with and support from various left-wing groups including Communists. The life of Henry A. Wallace is not one story, but four.

Henry A. Wallace's interest in breeding corn began when his father invited George Washington Carver, the famous scientist who was attending Iowa State College where Henry's father taught to visit the Wallace home. Wallace, who was six years old at the time, later said that Carver had taught him an appreciation for plants that he would never forget. At the turn of the century, while still in high school, Wallace began experimenting with corn to develop a hybrid that would produce a superior yield.

Between 1893 and 1910, Iowa farmers tried to grow corn that looked good. Corn shows were held throughout the state to which each farmer could send twelve of his prettiest ears to be judged. What was important was to have cylindrical ears with straight rows of wedge-shaped kernels. Individual ears of corn that won top prizes at such shows would sell for up to $250 to farmers who wanted to use the ear as seed for next year's crop. But since corn grown from a prize seed would usually be pollinated by a non-prize-winning corn, there was no assurance that a champion ear would produce the same good-looking corn the next year. But more importantly, Wallace realized that the way corn looked did not necessarily have anything to do with the amount of corn a seed might yield and increasing the yield was what would benefit farmers the most.

Hybrid seed is developed by crossing two different types of corn, each one of which has been inbred by pollinating the silk of a plant with pollen taken only from its own male component, the tassel. The inbred corn will have certain characteristics such as high yield or vigorous growth. By crossing the two inbred types,

The patriarch Wallace, "Uncle" Henry.
—COURTESY OF STATE HISTORI-
CAL SOCIETY OF IOWA

a hybrid may be produced that has both high yield and vigorous growth. While other boys in high school were playing ball, fishing, or studying, Henry A. Wallace was planting, thinning, cultivating, and detasseling five acres of corn behind his house.

Wallace continued his experiments after his graduation from Iowa State College in 1910. During this time, he also began writing for the family paper. He produced his first hybrid seed in 1913. Because space in his family's yard was limited, he later used land on the farm of Simon Casady, Jr., and on a farm owned by the Wallace family in Johnston, which was tenant-farmed by Jay Newlin.

In 1926, with some Des Moines businessmen, Wallace founded the Hi-Bred Corn Company, the first business to research, develop, produce, and sell hybrid seed corn. Along with such seed companies as DeKalb, Cargill, Pfister, and Funk, Hi-Bred Corn Company (its name was later changed to Pioneer Hi-Bred Corn Company) changed the face of the Iowa farm.

In 1934, only 2 percent of Iowa's cornfields were planted with hybrid corn seed. By 1944, 99.8 percent of Iowa's corn fields were planted with hybrid corn seed as compared with 59 percent for the country as a whole. During the same period, the average corn yield in Iowa jumped from 21.9 to 31.9 bushels per acre. By the year 2000, yield had increased to more than 100 bushels per acre. This was not all due directly to hybridization but also to the development of commercial fertilizer and technological improvements in planting and harvesting. However, both fertilization and technological improvements were made possible by the use of hybrid corn seed. In 1997, 20 percent of the Pioneer Hi-Bred Corn Company, which was started on money borrowed from Henry A. Wallace's wife in 1926 and until 1930 consisted only of Wallace, Casady, Newlin, and a few unpaid employees, was sold to the chemical giant DuPont. Two years later the remaining 80 percent was sold to DuPont for $7.7 billion.

Wallace's role as a scientist in changing the face of American farming was significant. But he also contributed to changing the face of American farming through *Wallace's Farmer*, a family publication that had been founded by his grandfather and edited by his father. Henry A. Wallace came from a line of Wallaces that had dedicated themselves to the improvement of the lot of the American farmer.

Henry A. Wallace's grandfather was Henry Wallace, a Presbyterian minister-turned-journalist who once spoke from his pulpit in favor of Lincoln's Emancipation Proclamation in spite of the opposition of his own church members. Speaking out for what he believed to be right regardless of the consequences was a trait that was passed down from Henry Wallace to his son and grandson. In 1877, Henry Wallace began writing a page on agriculture in his local paper in Winterset so that he could preach his views on better farming and better living. He urged crop rotation and the use of new varieties of crops; he appealed to farmers to use the power of the ballot box to defeat legislators who did not serve their interests; and he encouraged attractive homes for the benefit of farmers' children. The page was well received, reprinted in more and more midwestern papers, and his readers affectionately began calling him "Uncle Henry." In 1883, he was asked to become editor of the *Iowa Homestead*, a position he held for twelve years.

Henry Wallace's oldest son, Henry C. Wallace (called "Harry" to avoid confusion with his father), was a farmer when he was asked to become assistant professor at Iowa State College. Shortly after arriving in Ames, Harry became a partner in publishing *The Farm and Dairy*. In 1895, the elder Henry Wallace was asked to leave the *Homestead* because of his criticisms of railroads and business for taking advantage of farmers. "Uncle Henry" was not able to sit still without a paper in which to express his views, so the Wallace family bought out Harry's partner and changed the name of *The Farm and Dairy* to *Wallaces' Farmer* and began publishing it weekly.

Wallaces' Farmer became second only to the Bible in the homes of Iowa farmers. In addition to farming news, it had a women's page and weekly Sunday school lessons. In 1896, when Henry A. Wallace was eight years old, his family moved from Ames to Des Moines so that his father, Harry, could become the paper's business manager. Uncle Henry developed a reputation for leadership and authority among farmers, and in 1908, President Theodore Roosevelt appointed him to the Country Life Commission, an investigative committee seeking to improve the rural sector of the American economy. In 1916, Uncle Henry died and the editorship of *Wallaces' Farmer* passed to Henry C. Wallace.

In addition to editing *Wallaces' Farmer*, Henry C. Wallace served in the administration of President Wilson and was later named secretary of agriculture under Warren G. Harding about eight months after a depression had struck farmers. Wallace said the problem was overproduction of farm crops, but no one would listen to him. When he finally began to be heard, Harding died and Wallace, who was also made secretary of agriculture under Calvin Coolidge, had to begin anew, preaching the need for controls on production.

Henry C. Wallace died unexpectedly in 1924, and Henry A. Wallace became editor, making the magazine into the most influential farm journal in the nation. Henry A. Wallace had seen his father's prediction of a farm depression come true. In 1921, the purchasing power of a farmer was just 78 percent of what it had been five years earlier. He felt that farmers would

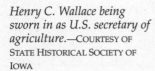
Henry C. Wallace being sworn in as U.S. secretary of agriculture.—COURTESY OF STATE HISTORICAL SOCIETY OF IOWA

need government assistance through limits on production. When it became clear that the Hoover administration would resist any such aid to farmers, Henry A. Wallace left the Republican Party and joined the Democrats. Through increased involvement in politics and the pulpit of the press, Wallace said over and over again that the cure for hard times "is simply that a greater percentage of the income of the nation be turned back to the mass of the people." He believed that production should be controlled and consumption increased.

For instance, Wallace tried to convince his readers to limit the cultivation of corn in favor of clover, but they did not follow through. He promoted international trade of agricultural commodities to increase the market for farm goods. This led him to advocate the cancellation of Germany's World War I reparations and of European war debts so that those countries could buy American corn and other farm products. He also advocated the reduction of high American tariffs. His goal was to improve the plight of the American farmer, a goal that would require a total social transformation. To Wallace, it was a social sin to allow a condition in which "whole classes of our people are impoverished at the same time as other classes are made rich."

In 1932, nearly ten years after Harding's death, Franklin Delano Roosevelt asked Henry A. Wallace to come to Washington to take the same position his father had held: secretary of agriculture. Wallace took the position with three principles: (1) a sincere belief in the dignity of the individual; (2) a sincere belief that American agriculture was in trouble because of its ability to overproduce and that a "planned scarcity" was necessary; and (3) a sincere commitment to small farmers who were helpless victims of conditions beyond their control.

He began his tenure as secretary of agriculture with vigor and enthusiasm. Roosevelt was inaugurated on March 4, 1933, and on March 10, Wallace presided at the opening meeting of a conference to draft new farm legislation to suggest an emergency session of Congress. During the next eight years, as the country experienced the Great Depression, Wallace assumed the role of ideologist for Roosevelt's New Deal. His goal was

Henry A. Wallace examining his hybrid corn.
—COURTESY OF STATE HISTORICAL SOCIETY OF IOWA

not just economic equality but social justice as well. Conservatives labeled him a dangerous radical, but Roosevelt chose Wallace to be his running mate for his third term as president. In 1940, Wallace was elected vice president under Roosevelt and gave up his editorial responsibilities at *Wallaces' Farmer*.

Because of political disagreements, Wallace was not chosen to run with Roosevelt for his fourth term as president. Instead, Harry S. Truman was tapped at the Democratic Convention to be the vice presidential candidate. Roosevelt died three months after his inauguration, making Truman president. If Roosevelt had died a few months earlier, Wallace would have become president of the United States. Instead, he was offered the cabinet post of secretary of commerce, a position he held for a year and a half in the Truman administration.

Wallace's increasing involvement in foreign affairs led to his dismissal as secretary of commerce. In 1946, he became editor of the *New Republic*, a position which he used to launch his bid for the presidency with the Progressive Party. He had a hatred of war and believed that international peace could be fostered by applying Christian principles to international relations. "The Kingdom of Heaven here on earth can only be attained when men in their politics, their daily work, their science, their art, their philosophy, and their religion are reaching out continuously for an even higher manifestation and appreciation of that blissful, unmanifested reality which we call God," he said.

Wallace's reputation was permanently damaged by his being a spokesman for the Progressive Party, because it attracted Communists, which cast a reputation for disloyalty on Wallace. Even though he repudiated the Progressive Party in 1950 and supported the U.S. action in Korea, Wallace could not undo the effect his association with it had on what people thought of him.

Henry A. Wallace's final years were spent running an experimental farm in Salem, New York. He was able to put the turmoil of politics behind him and return to his first love: experimenting with the development of varieties of plants.

Henry Wallace, Henry C. Wallace, and Henry A. Wallace were all remarkable men dedicated to serving others. Their credo was found on the masthead of *Wallaces' Farmer*: "Good Farming—Clear Thinking—Right Living." It was also summed up in a speech made by Henry A. Wallace in 1943: "Christianity is not star gazing for foolish idealism. Applied on a worldwide scale, it is intensely practical. Bread cast upon the waters does return." His crusade for social reform was guided by the moral precepts of Jesus' Sermon on the Mount, carried out through an understanding of economics, and implemented by political means. He never wavered from his purpose of serving humanity.

Four generations of Henry Wallaces. Counter clockwise from right are Henry Wallace ("Uncle" Henry, 1836–1916), Henry Cantwell Wallace ("Harry," 1866–1924), Henry Agard Wallace (1888–1965), and Henry Browne Wallace (H. B. 1915–   ).—COURTESY OF STATE HISTORICAL SOCIETY OF IOWA

Part 5
Mavericks and Strays

19
Buffalo Bill
Killer

A single glance at the face of Isaac Cody was enough to see that something terrible had happened. Pale and shaking, he pushed open the door of a cabin in Scott County and moaned: "Sam's dead!"

Sam's brother Bill, seven years his junior, never forgot that electrifying announcement. When he heard it, he was old enough to realize that Sam was not a skilled rider but had been under the impression that his brother could handle any horse on the farm. Before Sam's broken body was brought into the cabin, Bill made a silent resolution—*He'd learn to ride so well that no horse would ever fall on him!*

His brother's untimely death was one of three turning points in the life of William Frederick Cody, who won international fame as Buffalo Bill. No one wanted to remain on the farm where Sam died, so Isaac took his pregnant wife and two living children to Kansas and settled not far from Fort Leavenworth. Isaac Cody tried his hand at driving a stage, but during the spring of 1857, he died suddenly. That did not affect eleven-year-old Bill's emotions as much as the loss of Sam, but the boy who had been taken out of Iowa found himself thrust into the role of family breadwinner.

He found a job of sorts with a supply train that accompanied citizen-soldiers who mounted a futile expedition against the Mormons. When that job petered out, Bill became a mounted messenger for a freight firm. In his spare time, he went to school long enough to learn to read short words and to write his name. After trying his hand at riding for the Pony Express, he had the

One of the last good photographs of Cody was made early in 1903.—ILLUSTRATED AND DRAMATIC NEWS

opportunity to become a scout, at age seventeen, with the Ninth Cavalry, U.S. Army. Bill reveled at having taken part in "real" fights against the Comanches and the Kiowas, and he enlisted in the army as soon as he was old enough.

After an uneventful period as a Union soldier late in the Civil War, the young fellow from Iowa experienced a second dramatic turning point. Out of the blue he was offered work that really suited him—killing buffalo. The buffalo were used to provide meat for the men who worked hard all day building the railroad. During a period of more than a year, he claimed to have downed at least half a dozen big animals every single day he hunted. Hence, the nickname of Buffalo Bill was given to him before he was old enough to have hair on his chin, and it stuck with him for the rest of his life. After killing buffalo, he went back to the army as the Fifth Cavalry's chief of scouts. Due to a bizarre chain of circumstances, the newcomer to Nebraska got elected to the legislature, but he shook his head at the news and was never seated. It was during this period that a third unexpected event changed the direction in which he was riding, and once Cody set his bearings on this trail he never swerved from it.

On a blustery day during the early fall, a stranger walked up to Buffalo Bill on the streets of Omaha, thrust out his hand and said, "I'm Ned Buntline, and I've been dying to get acquainted with you." By 1869, even Buffalo Bill knew a little about this fellow from the East. Edward Zane Carroll Judson of Stamford, New York, earlier sensed that the time was ripe to begin exploiting tales of adventures in the West. Writing under the pseudonym Ned Buntline, which quickly became a household word, he is widely regarded today as having been "the father of the dime novel." His mother lode of yarns had been worked pretty thoroughly, so he wanted new material from Buffalo Bill.

The celebrated Buffalo Bill hunting his namesake.—Samuel Carter, *Illustrated London News*

Buffalo Bill with Sitting Bull in Montreal, 1885.—COURTESY OF BUFFALO BILL HISTORICAL CENTER

A few weeks after Ned went back East, a series of cliff-hangers that featured Buffalo Bill began appearing in the *New York Weekly*. As soon as these were put together into paperback novels, which really sold for a dime, the fellow who spent his early boyhood in Scott County found himself a celebrity. He knew that practically all of the tales were fictional, but the readers didn't.

Gen. Philip Sheridan of Civil War fame was not the sort of man to read himself to sleep with a dime novel, but his U.S. Army friends had told him a lot about Cody. In 1871, Sheridan invited the famous buffalo killer for an elaborate "outing" on the plains. Notables in the party included James Gordon Bennett, editor of the *New York Herald*; Charles L. Wilson of the *Chicago Evening Journal*; and a score of high-ranking military officers. Buffalo Bill guided these men and sixteen baggage wagons for 194 miles. During this "outing," these men, mostly from the East, killed about six hundred buffalo and two hundred elk.

The expedition generated so much publicity that soon after it ended its scout and leader was employed by Sheridan to arrange a "royal" buffalo hunt whose most noted member would be the Grand Duke Alexis, son of Russian Czar Alexander I. For this hunt Buffalo Bill hired a Sioux chieftain, Spotted Tail, to bring one hundred warriors into camp to stage a war dance for the Russian prince. Among the army officers who escorted the party was Gen. George A. Custer—barely four years away from the famous battle at the Little Big Horn. Once Buffalo Bill was confident that the prince had learned how to handle a rifle, he let him ride his own horse, Buckskin Joe, on a hunt. A story in the *New York Herald* labeled Cody as "guide, tutor, and entertaining agent" of the expedition.

Aspiring playwright Fred Meader of New York, who knew nothing of the celebrated buffalo hunter except what he read in newspapers and dime novels, adapted Ned Buntline's yarns into a drama that he called *Buffalo Bill, King of the Border Men*. As a melodrama, it wasn't much; yet it was enough to persuade Buntline that he had overlooked a prominent vein of gold. When Meader's work was rewritten as *Scouts of the Plains*, Buffalo Bill agreed to take to the stage as its star. It was just one short step from the stage to a big tent; when the Iowa native took that step, Buffalo Bill's Wild West Show opened in Chicago in 1872. Wild Bill Hickok, who helped to get the show on the road, soon quit.

Buffalo Bill left the sawdust trail briefly during the Sioux War of 1875–76 and brought some of Buntline's fiction to life. Since he was famous as a killer of buffalo and Indians, he may have reasoned, he had to play a real-life role that wouldn't disappoint his fans. During early July 1876, he helped to track a band of "renegade" Cheyennes to Wyoming's War Bonnet Creek. At a point not far from the Red Cloud agency, he fought it out with Yellow Hand (aka Yellow Hair), son of the noted chieftain Cut-Nose. When word of the skirmish reached reporters, they instantly labeled it as "the most daring fight ever to take place on American soil."

This fresh infusion of fame brought hordes to the Wild West Show during the following season. Buffalo Bill replaced Hickok with Annie Oakley, or "Little Sure Shot," and the famous chieftain Sitting Bull. His simulated Indian fights, cowboy shootouts, and buffalo hunts ran continuously for the next quarter-century. Despite the fact that the show drew capacity crowds that included heads of state, it failed to make its creator rich. He spent lavishly on wine and women and kept hiring dozens of persons he didn't really need until he had an entourage that at its peak numbered about five hundred persons.

Less than a generation after he had helped to found the Wyoming city that bears his name, the Wild West Show tumbled into bankruptcy in Denver. Buffalo Bill then launched a motion picture company to produce a film on the Indian wars. Although the film played in England and on the Continent for two four-year periods, Buffalo Bill managed to lose everything he made. He was a sure shot with a rifle and one of the greatest showmen of the century, but he never managed to hit the financial bull's eye. Buffalo Bill died in Colorado with only a few dollars in his pocket and no assets.

After he was buried close to the top of Lookout Mountain, the place became such a tourist mecca that far-sighted devotees built the Buffalo Bill Historical Center in Cody, Wyoming. Today it holds one of the nation's best exhibitions based on the colorful period during which buffalo were all but exterminated and the Indian-hating cowboys who were quickest on the draw briefly ruled boom towns of the West.

20
Black Hawk
Predator

"A six-foot male must have looked as though he had been to the makeup department, ready to assume a role in a movie or TV drama," a modern analyst concluded after becoming familiar with a person who spent much of his life in Iowa.

"He had a decidedly hooked nose plus hollow cheeks. His head would have made you think of Kojack. Except for a wee tuft of hair top center, his noggin seemed to have been shaved.

"Wearing a bright blanket over buckskin, the tanned skin of a sparrow hawk— complete with feathers—hung at his side. Had he been center stage a few years ago, he could have been credited with having launched a fad. Every time he moved his head, little baubles jingled from their positions in rows along the rim of each of his ears."

This eye-catching fellow is famous for having issued a pronouncement that struck dread into many who learned of it. "I hope I may not be obliged to dig up my Hatchet," he said. "I know these Long Knives have sweet tongues and fear they have cheated us all." That verdict, issued in the aftermath of the 1815 Treaty of Portage des Sioux, came from a Native American leader living on or near Rock River in present-day Illinois.

When he learned that the Missouri Sac and the Fox Indians had signed a treaty, the Winnebago-Sac Black Hawk, as he was called by the Long Knives (white men equipped with swords), was troubled and angry. Tribesmen knew him as Ma-ka-tai-me-she-kia-kiak, or Black Sparrow Hawk. The secretary of war told President James Madison that failure of the Rock River Sac to enter into the treaty could mean trouble.

Soldiers and settlers had been dealing with bands of Sac and other tribesmen of the middle Mississippi River region for more than a decade. In 1804 five of their leaders met with William Henry Harrison at St. Louis and entered into an agreement with him. Under its terms, the United States gained title to more than fifty-one million acres located largely in what is now western Illinois and Wisconsin. This transaction cost the young nation $2,234.50 in trade goods; a perpetual annuity in the sum of one thousand dollars was also promised in return for vast tracts of forests and rich farmland.

Members of the Pottawatomi tribe protested to Madison, claiming that "no part of the Illinois River does or ever did belong to the Sacs who sold it." Black Hawk, whose tribesmen formed a different band of Sacs, later insisted that the Native American leaders who entered into the transaction were drunk at the time. This treaty of 1804, he said many times, "was at the bottom of all the trouble [between white men and Rock River Sacs]."

Perpetually fuming at what he considered to be an injustice to tribesmen, the man named for the sparrow hawk became a

At the Battle of Bad Axe, a cannon mounted on the steamer Warrior *played havoc with insurgent native Americans.*

predator of large game when the War of 1812 broke out. Black Hawk formed an alliance with the British, and they may have given him a semi-official commission as a general.

Swooping down on isolated bands of Americans, this Sac and his followers kept part of the northwestern frontier in commotion. Some of the more significant clashes in which they participated under the leadership of Tecumseh took place at Frenchtown, Fort Stephenson, and Fort Meigs.

Black Hawk, who had the loan of several British cannons, once turned these pieces upon Zachary Taylor's force and won a quick victory for which Taylor never forgave him. It is still doubtful whether the Sac leader—never officially a chieftain— was present when Tecumseh was killed at the Battle of the Thames.

In the aftermath of the little war won by Americans, much of the land acquired in the treaty of 1804 was offered to veterans of the War of 1812 as bounty for their military service. During this period, Black Hawk participated in another parley. Describing it to an interpreter years afterward, the Sac leader said that: "Here, for the first time, I touched the goose quill to the treaty— not knowing, however, that by that act I consented to give away my village." By "touching the goose quill," Black Hawk, who could neither read nor write, gave the assent of his people to the St. Louis treaty that had been effected more than a decade earlier by Harrison.

Always insisting that he had been tricked, Black Hawk had consented to leave behind the Rock River Sac lands, including a village so old that no man knew when it was established. Situated upon what a white historian described as "a lovely neck of land made by the union of the Rock with the Mississippi River," the village included more than one hundred lodges. Gentle slopes covered with lush grass and adorned by fine trees led upward to a chain of tiny tree-covered hills. Fort Armstrong, built on the southern tip of Rock Island, was barely visible in the distance.

During a single season, agents of John Jacob Astor's American Fur Company collected at Rock Island 500 mink skins, 2,760 beaver, almost 1,000 otter, more than 13,000 raccoon and nearly as many muskrat, 700 bear, and nearly 30,000 deer. In addition, they received from tribesmen more than 250,000 pounds of deer tallow plus 1,000 pounds of beeswax and 3,000 pounds of feathers. For these commodities, they gave blankets, calicoes, rifles, shotguns, gunpowder, kettles of copper and brass, needles and thread, and a few horses.

For more generations than any man could count, the Sac disposed of their dead in and around their village. A white commentator ascribed much of their reluctance to go to the Iowa River region to these graves writing that:

> As a paramount religious duty, they feed the spirits of their ancestors at stated times, for whose use to light these ghostly banquets they believed the moon to have been made. The Indians decorate and make moan over the graves as long as they live.

Whites who bragged that "the only good Indian is a dead Indian" ignored traditions of their foes and began demanding that the Rock River Sac abandon their tribal lands. The Corn Treaty of 1816 actually did require them and their Fox allies to move to designated regions along the Iowa River.

Small and scattered bands of U.S. Army soldiers clashed with Native Americans for years after whites believed that a full agreement had been reached. In 1828, when the patience of settlers was exhausted, soldiers drove the tribesmen across the Mississippi River and ordered them to settle in what is now Iowa.

Black Hawk never pretended to comply with orders, except under force. Advised by Waubesheik (also known as White Cloud), a mustache-wearing nephew who claimed to have prophetic powers, he sent runners to leaders of other tribes. Surely it would be possible to form an anti-American league somewhat like that effected earlier by Tecumseh, White Cloud (also known as the Prophet) reasoned. One by one, the bands with whom Black Hawk hoped to make an alliance turned him down: first the Winnebago, then the Pottawatomi and the Kickapoo. He knew better than to attempt to make a deal with the Sioux; these mortal enemies of his people would have scorned the idea of a parley.

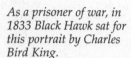

As a prisoner of war, in 1833 Black Hawk sat for this portrait by Charles Bird King.

During each spring of the first three years he was in Iowa, Black Hawk and his son Kanonecan ("Youngest of the Thunders") led his people back across the great river to plant corn in their ancestral lands. Settlers who had homesteads in the region were both frightened and angry. They sent one appeal after another to Washington until in 1832 a military force was organized. Its appearance on the frontier marked the beginning of the episode known as the Black Hawk War. Measured by later standards, it was only a series of very small hostile encounters between armed forces.

Volunteers from numerous Illinois towns and villages converged upon the Mississippi River at Dixon's Ferry where Gen. Henry Atkinson (known to Indians as the White Beaver) and other U.S. Army officers were waiting for them with the Second, Fifth, and Sixth Regiments of the U.S. Army. Combat was launched when Black Hawk equipped some of his warriors with a white flag and sent them to parley with their foes. Untrained members of the militia fired on the men who had come to talk about a truce and killed two of them. Black Hawk told his followers that was how the Long Knives always acted and launched sporadic predatory raids. He managed to seize a few cattle, a war party captured two white women and briefly held them captive, and as the Sac retreated westward there were occasional clashes with members of the force assembled by the white men.

In late June, Maj. John Dement was attacked by a band of Sac at Kellogg's Grove. Black Hawk later recalled killing several men and about forty horses; he lost two young chiefs and seven warriors. Young braves were eager to follow up by attacking, but Black Hawk persuaded them not to waste their powder as they "had already run the bear into his hole"—or had forced their enemies to return to their camp. It was about this time that a party of Winnebago passed by, returning some young white women who had been taken captive by Sacs.

Weeks after being forced into a largely defensive role, Black Hawk and his warriors made camp near the mouth of the Bad Axe River. When he found that pursuing foes had added a small gunboat to their fire power, he recognized it as the *Warrior* and rejoiced that he knew her captain. He sent a messenger to the river with a small piece of white cotton cloth on a pole, hoping for a truce. A Winnebago aboard the vessel warned the Sacs: "Run and hide, the whites are going to shoot!" They were right; in the only skirmish of any significance, the Battle of the Bad Axe, an estimated 150 braves were killed. A dispatch to Gen. Winfield Scott notified him that U.S. casualties numbered twenty-four, of whom only six were killed.

About two hundred men, women, and children escaped by swimming across the Mississippi River, but both Black Hawk and the Prophet were captured. Wearing handcuffs, a shackle, and a ball and chain, the Sac leader was taken to St. Louis and then transferred to Fortress Monroe in Virginia. Forced to enter into a treaty, the captive had no land to surrender except large tracts along the Iowa River.

On September 21, 1832, the agreement transferred most of this land to whites in return for promises of cash, blacksmith service, tobacco, and salt. Though not nearly as large as some

Photographed at Tamo, Iowa, about 1860, this Fox grave indicates how Black Hawk was buried more than a generation earlier.

other transactions of the period, the land acquired by the United States was big enough to form the nucleus of another state—Iowa. A then-famous, half-breed interpreter, Antoine Le Claire, helped the parties reach an agreement and was rewarded with two sections of land (1,280 acres).

The following spring, the captives were returned to Iowa and released as a result of orders issued by President Andrew Jackson. It was there that Black Hawk began dictating his autobiography to Le Claire and completed it in the "tenth moon" of 1833. Soon widely hailed as an American classic, the volume issued before the year ended briefly made the aging warrior a celebrity. At his death in 1838 at his lodge on the Des Moines River, he was "laid away" in Sac fashion in a reclining posture beneath a wooden shelter, and by his side were placed the many gifts—swords, canes, and medals—which had been given to him.

Except in Illinois and Iowa, the Black Hawk War would today be only a minor footnote to the history of the first half of the nineteenth century were it not for the opponents whom

Black Hawk and his warriors faced. White forces led by Atkinson included future Civil War Generals Alfred E. Johnston and Robert Anderson, who soared to fame at Fort Sumter, South Carolina. A contingent of Illinois volunteers reached Rock Island on May 7, shortly after Zachary Taylor took command of its Fort Armstrong. Among these fledgling fighting men was an awkward twenty-three year old, who stood six feet four inches tall and had been elected captain of his company. At least twice, officers among the professional soldiers punished this volunteer's minor infractions by making him wear a wooden sword for a day or two. On July 10, after two brief re-enlistments, the military service of Abraham Lincoln came to an end. The future commander of over 3.5 million Union soldiers had not fired a single shot at an enemy but somehow managed to lose his horse and was forced to walk most of the way home.

Among the officers who escorted the Sac captives to St. Louis was a young lieutenant named Jefferson Davis, who then did not have the faintest idea that he and Lincoln would one day direct their respective armies from rival capitals less than one hundred miles apart. Reflecting upon the "little war" in later years, Davis pointed out that it took four thousand whites to defeat five hundred Indians who were encumbered by their families. "The real heroes of this struggle," Davis wrote, "were Black Hawk and his warriors."

Though that verdict never gained wide acceptance, it was the Sac leader Black Hawk who, among the forty-five hundred who fought in 1832, gained an intangible but lasting memorial. It was his impact upon the region that led to adoption of "The Hawkeye State" as a nickname for Iowa.

21
Grant Wood

American Gothic

A painting rarely makes news at the time it is executed. Even if the artist is internationally famous, interest in the unveiling of a new work is usually confined to a relatively small circle of art critics and art lovers. An exception to this rule, *American Gothic* triggered numerous newspaper stories soon after it was completed and widely reproduced in 1932. Most verdicts concerning the painting were strongly worded, and they were almost equally divided between glowing praise and harsh denunciation.

Even the most ardent admirers of Grant Wood acknowledged that his later painting entitled *Daughters of Revolution* caused viewers to split into two widely divided camps. "Grant Wood should spend a few years at a good art school, learning both technique and good manners," a New England critic wrote. "He has produced a trio of expressionless faces that constitute a mockery of the American Revolution and all patriots who honor its memory." Far to the south, a delighted writer for a New Orleans newspaper told readers that "an artist from Iowa...has produced a lasting commentary upon some of the most absurd attitudes and practices of many a person in our nation...." Heads and shoulders of three females, one of whom holds a blue-on-white cup of bone china, constitute the foreground. In each case, the mouth of the lady depicted constitutes a thin vertical line. Two of the tight-lipped figures wear glasses, and not one has the faintest trace of an expression on her face. Only the title plus a careful look at their surroundings reveal that these are ramrod conservative members of the Daughters of the American Revolution (D.A.R.).

At the University of Iowa, artist in residence Grant Wood became known as the first great regional painter in America.
—COURTESY OF UNIVERSITY OF IOWA

Behind the ladies hangs a framed copy of the familiar masterpiece of German-born American artist Emanuel Leutze, *George Washington crossing the Delaware River.* Although Leutze greatly admired Washington and painted it as a tribute to our first president's skill as a military strategist, the famous work is full of major errors. It shows the head of the Continental Army moving toward British Redcoats in broad daylight rather than soon after midnight on December 26, 1776. Also, although the crossing was made in a huge and clumsy boat built to transport ore, Leutze showed Washington standing upright in a vessel of conventional design.

No doubt about it, Grant Wood knew what he was doing when he selected that famous work of art for inclusion in his own painting. Newspapers, magazines, and books whose editors elected to reproduce only a portion of Wood's work sometimes chopped the figure of Washington in half; when that is done, the message of the Iowa artist loses much of its punch. As clearly as any masterpiece that came from the brush of a man who grew up on a farm close to Animosa, *Daughters* is undiluted satire. Now that it has become widely known, however, an occasional member of the D.A.R. professes to see it as a tribute to their organization.

Wood, who habitually kept a half-smile on his face after he became artist-in-residence at the University of Iowa in 1935, would probably guffaw at the fashion in which some of his paintings are now interpreted—or misinterpreted. Whether he deliberately produced jigsaw puzzles from which some pieces

Conspicuous in the background, Washington Crossing the Delaware is essential to the message of Daughters of Revolution.—CINCINNATI ART MUSEUM

are missing or whether this aspect of his work is an inadvertent byproduct of his distinctive style, no one knows for sure.

When following a plow during adolescent years, the youngster decided that he did not intend to spend his life growing corn. He valued Iowa's rich black farmland so greatly that his attitude toward it approached reverence, but Grant "had a queer kind of itch in his head and his hands" that made him want to do creative work. He studied for a period at the Minneapolis School of Design and Handicraft and impressed instructors with his special brand of manual dexterity. Though he didn't have a patron then or ever, he somehow managed to spend time at the Art Institute of Chicago and the Academie Julian in Paris.

Approaching age thirty, the Iowa artist found exactly the job he wanted. For a five-year period beginning in 1919, he taught art in the public schools of Cedar Rapids. When a spacious Memorial Building for the city was on the drawing board, Wood was commissioned to create a stained glass window for it. Always a perfectionist, he set out for Germany to find skilled craftsmen almost as soon as he accepted the job.

While in Germany and other parts of Europe, Wood spent much of his time viewing original paintings—not reproductions—by men who had flourished four hundred years earlier. He came home saying that he would never forget their "stark realism." Having also been influenced by the style of more recent German artists, he set out to put on canvas some realistic but formal scenes with which he was intimately familiar. That meant, of course, that he set out to paint the Iowa countryside out of sheer love.

Legend says that a casual acquaintance, who knew Wood sometimes got ideas from photographs, gave him a stack of old pictures. Among these images was one that showed a two-story residence in Eldon that was locally renowned because it had a gothic window near the comb of its roof. Though it was relatively inconspicuous in the photograph, that window proved to be an inspiration to the artist. Using it as a backdrop, he depicted a man and a woman standing in front of it in such fashion that the window looms into prominence. Like the women in *Daughters of Revolution,* which he produced later, the two persons depicted in Wood's *American Gothic* stand stiffly erect, and their faces are severely expressionless. A three-pronged pitchfork is held in the right hand of the male, whose open coat reveals rough clothing such as a farmer might don on Sunday when going to church.

There is no evidence that Grant Wood labored longer over this painting than numerous others that came from his brush. Yet within a few decades it was heralded as "the most widely viewed work by an American artist." To millions of people who found it interesting or magnetic, it has come to symbolize not simply Iowa and her people but the entire Midwest.

Still recognizable at a glance, *American Gothic* has accumulated its special set of riddles. Since the artist didn't think it necessary to stipulate who the persons in the painting were, critics and analysts soon divided on this matter. Approximately half of the art books and reference works in which the painting is reproduced inform viewers that Wood painted a farmer and his wife. Logical as this conclusion seems to be, the other half of the volumes in which the paint-

Having been reproduce many hundreds of times, American Gothic is regarded as the most familiar work of art by an American.
—ART INSTITUTE OF CHICAGO

ing appears say that the man and woman are an Iowa farmer and his daughter.

Purchased by the Friends of Art for presentation to the Art Institute of Chicago, the painting is among the Institute's prized possessions. *American Gothic* brought fame to its creator and to his state, and other less famous works by Wood are scattered all the way from New York's Metropolitan Museum of Art to Omaha's Joslyn Art Museum.

Part of the mystery—and the perennial magnetism—of Wood's work lies in the fact that viewers still react to it in widely different fashions. Numerous analysts are of the opinion that most, if not all, of Wood's paintings are deliberately sardonic. Yet in his *Iowa — A History*, Joseph F. Wall sees Wood's body of work as constituting a portrait of the state:

> Its farm couples standing in gothic angularity; its small towns peopled with Daughters of the American Revolution; and the land itself, not flat, but softly round and fecund—all permanently delineated, so that the New York motorist speeding across Iowa on Interstate 80 will glance out his window

Young Corn. *Grant Wood, 1931. Oil on masonite panel, 23½ x
29⅞ inches. Copyright Cedar Rapids, Iowa, Community School
District. Memorial to Lennie Schloeman, Woodrow Wilson School.*

and say, "Why it looks just like a Grant Wood painting," surprised to discover that nature frequently follows art.

Regardless of what Grant Wood wanted viewers to see in
his paintings, there's no debate about the subject matter with
which he worked. Nearly all of his best-known canvases are 100
percent Iowa, for he found inspiration wherever he looked. His
Young Corn, completed in 1931, was soon featured in *Art Digest*.
During a period spent as founder of an art colony at Stone City,
he surveyed the surrounding countryside and put it on canvas
in unique fashion.

Only one notable native of the region is known to have been
a trifle scornful of Wood's canvasses, regardless of whether they
are sardonic or realistic. Herbert Hoover took one look at the
painting depicting his birthplace and snorted, "Entirely too
elaborate!"

22
Wyatt Earp

O. K. Corral

"We hadn't been in town a week before I knew there was something queer about the whole place. I had barely turned two, so it took me a while to figure out what it was. Now I know that I wasn't cut out to be a Dutchman."

As soon as they got settled in their new home in Pella, Nicholas Earp realized that his small son didn't like it, but he knew of no other place within striking distance where he could get a quarter section of land for nearly nothing. By 1850, most of the best farmland in what is now the Midwest was moving up in price.

Immigrants from the Netherlands settled Wyatt Earp's boyhood home three years before he arrived and gave it a name meaning "place of refuge." Their wagons had hardly stopped rolling before they started to plant tulips. By the time the grist mill was running and the blacksmith shop was nearly finished, the place looked as though it had been picked up and moved from Europe. Dislike for the "foreign-lookin'" town probably accounted for the fact that adjoining land was still cheap.

Before he turned twelve, Wyatt set out to do something about things in Pella. He confided to his father that he was going to organize a club and be the head honcho. The boy didn't say that he planned to limit membership to a couple of his brothers and a few other boys whose clothing and speech didn't instantly identify them as Dutch.

By the time Wyatt's club had held two or three meetings, a new boy arrived straight from the Old Country. Pete Gaas spoke only a few words of English, but he managed to let it be

Even during his years as a buffalo skinner, Wyatt looked like he'd just arrived from the East when he sat for a photographer.

known that he wanted to join the club. When its barefoot leader shook his head and pointed to the open door of the barn where they were meeting, Pete didn't leave. Instead, he stamped all over Wyatt's toes with his wooden shoes. Earp, who never forgot that boyhood incident, once told an acquaintance that he reckoned that was what helped him decide to strike out on his own mighty early.

After he'd been gone from home for most of a day during the spring of 1862, his father missed him and organized a search party. Somebody found him at the recruitment office in Ottumwa. He had already gone on record as dying to fight the Rebels and was trying hard to persuade an officer that he had turned eighteen but was mighty small for his age.

It suited Wyatt just fine when his family hitched up with a wagon train whose trail boss said they wouldn't stop until they reached California. Since they'd have to go through Sioux country, the sixteen-year-old boy oiled and polished the hunting rifle that he handled better than most grown men. When half of the horses gave out before they got across Kansas, Wyatt lit out on his own— just like he'd been wanting to do since he was knee high to a duck. He drove a stagecoach until he got tired of sitting all the time, then tried his hand guarding a party of surveyors. Soon after he turned up in Kansas City, Wild Bill Hickok confided to him that there was a good market for buffalo hides, so he hunted for a while. Nearly every time he had a load of skins to sell, he tried a different cow town. That's how he turned up in Ellsworth, Kansas, close to the northern end of the Chisholm Trail.

The buffalo hunter had been in the Grand Central Hotel only a couple of days when Ben and Bill Thompson hit town. These thirsty cowhands soon got into a fracas with the sheriff. Before it was over Chauncey B. Whitney took a load of buckshot in his chest, and Bill Thompson lit out for Texas. His brother stayed behind with plenty of ammunition and dared anybody to come near him.

By the time Wyatt reached Dodge, saloons on Front Street featured Prickly Ash Bitters.

*Sheriff William B. ("Bat")
Masterson was briefly
Earp's superior.*

Mayor Jim Miller still had a marshal and two deputies on hand, but he didn't quite know what to do with them. Wyatt Earp sauntered across the street from the hotel, found the mayor, and allowed as how somebody out to get a gun and arrest Ben Thompson or "fill him full of lead." On the spot, the town official pinned a badge on the stranger and told him to go after Thompson. It took him all of ten minutes to make an arrest; telling the story later, he explained: "That's how I got into the law business."

Since his reputation preceded him to Wichita, Mayor Jim Hope made Earp a deputy marshal before he had a chance to think things over and maybe turn down the job. It was even tamer than driving a stage or skinning buffalo. In Wichita, the man whose formative years were spent in peaceful Iowa was applauded when he appeared at the door of Ida May's "parlor," pushing a piano the madam had neglected to pay for. When widely feared Shanghai Pierce "hurrahed all night," the town marshal took him by the collar and escorted him to the calaboose without a fight.

Consumptive dentist John Henry ("Doc") Holliday wielded a shotgun at the O.K. Corral.

When the Jones and Plummer Trail was opened, Dodge City began to boom at Wichita's expense. Mayor George M. Hoover made Earp an offer he couldn't resist—he could be second in authority only to Sheriff Bat Masterson. Pay would be $250 a month plus $2.50 for each arrest made, the mayor added. Wyatt rode into "the wickedest little city in the U.S.A." about the time Big Nose Kate Fisher began getting rich from her girls and famous actor Eddie Foy was planning to put on a show.

Dodge was a haven for ex-soldiers, cowhands, prostitutes, railroad workers, buffalo hunters, and faro dealers. Many of them didn't like the way the new marshal went about his business, so they got $1,000 together and offered it as bounty to anyone who'd send the lawman to Boot Hill.

No one collected the bounty, and he had it out in the street with only one man, who crumpled into the dirt at Wyatt's third shot. Leaving Dodge for no good reason except that he was restless again, the man who didn't like Pella was joined by his brothers Virgil, Morgan, and James. This foursome turned up in Tombstone, Arizona Territory, and this time it was Virgil who became a marshal. James bought part interest in a saloon, Morgan began riding shotgun on a stage, and Wyatt put his life on the line nightly by dealing faro at a saloon.

Virgil soon butted heads with Billy Clanton, a part-time rustler who vowed that he, his brother, and his friends wouldn't put up with a town curfew. After the forces of law and order clashed with gunslingers three or four times, the Clantons and the McLaurys rode into town on October 26, 1881, looking for trouble. Unlike Belle Starr's organized gang of hoodlums who tried to avoid the Earps, these fellows were ordinary cowpokes who hated badges. Their arrival precipitated the famous fight at the O.K. Corral, which was an eight-man duel. The defenders, Wyatt, two of his brothers, and Doc Holliday, took three nonfatal slugs, but the meeting at the corral ended when Billy Clanton, Frank McLaury, and his brother Tom McLaury were hauled off feet first.

Though it was no more remarkable or deadly than dozens of other brawls in cow towns, a fictionalized biography of Wyatt Earp elevated this gunfight to unequaled prominence. Hollywood took to the brief cowboy era like a duck takes to water, and in 1946, John Ford persuaded Henry Fonda to play Wyatt Earp in *My Darling Clementine*. A decade later Burt Lancaster, Kirk Douglas, Rhonda Fleming, and Jo Ann Fleet starred in the *Gunfight at the O.K. Corral*, and the fellow who got into the law and order business by accident became the most noted of cow town marshals.

For years, descendants of the immigrants who made Pella a tiny "island of Europe" on the plains refused to take seriously the fame of the boy who ran away because he wanted to fight in a blue uniform. Today, however, Pella's historical village on Franklin Street offers visitors a chance to tour Wyatt Earp's boyhood home.

For information about it, call (515) 628-2409.

Part 6
The Limelight

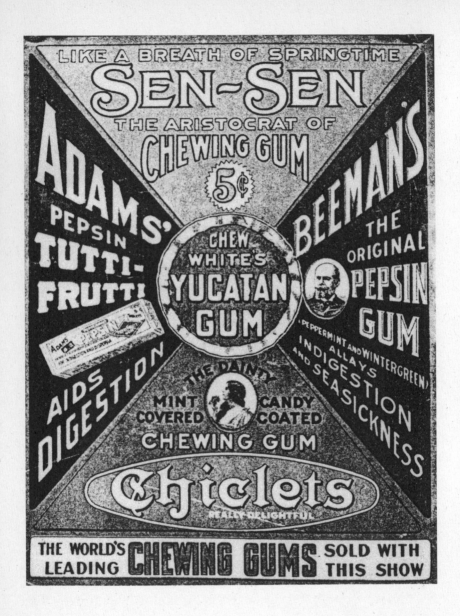

23
Five Ringlings
Showmen Without Equal

Dan Rice is not commonly remembered today, but in the aftermath of the Civil War, he was heralded as one of the nation's greatest entertainers. He conceived the novel idea of traveling up and down the Mississippi River on a steamboat with his Great Paris Pavilion of animals and performers. Late one afternoon, the steamboat docked at McGregor, Iowa. Dan's best horse, a black animal that performed several crowd-pleasing tricks, had somehow managed to snap the leather straps that allowed the acrobat to stay on his back.

With a show scheduled for the following day, Rice sent roustabouts to scour the town in search of somebody—anybody—who knew how to handle leather. Rice was almost resigned to the fact that the show would have to be staged without its most celebrated act. He was delighted, however, when a harness maker who was able to fix the straps was found. Before the performing horse was led on deck he gave three tickets to the fellow, a German immigrant.

That evening the man gave the tickets to his wife and grunted, "Somebody will have to stay home; we can't afford to pay admission." Twelve-year-old Otto is said to have put up such a howl that his father and mother decided to take him to the show, leaving his older brothers behind to watch over the younger boys.

Otto was so enthralled by the performance that within a few days he had persuaded his brothers to help him sew scraps of cloth together to make a tent. At age six, Charles was better than passable as a fiddler; two of the older boys danced after a fashion, and Otto could sing without music. With their talents pooled and the tent finished, in 1870, the Ringling brothers offered townsfolk entertainment by their Classic and Comic Concert Company. A trained goat, the only animal, stole the show, and the enterprising brothers grossed $8.39 from their first performance.

Al had a yen to become a juggler, so he spent his spare time tossing balls into the air. John told his four older brothers in no uncertain terms that *he* was going to be the clown. By the time the family moved to Baraboo, Wisconsin, juvenile plans and skills had matured a bit, so they gave performances everywhere they could get a crowd together. At the end of their first season they had a profit of nearly three hundred dollars to split and had decided to go into the circus business.

Their boyish enthusiasm might have waned or disappeared entirely had they known that most of the general public considered a circus to be the lowest form of entertainment. After admitting that some Americans considered "the clown of the circus to be the greatest man living," a writer for *Amusements* magazine mocked these folk. "To them," he wrote, "the climax of pleasure is to visit a filthy menagerie of half-dead animals in a reeky day in July and sit for hours giggling at monkeys in caps and jackets riding ponies."

Charles F. Browne, who used Artemus Ward as his pseudonym when he wrote what was then considered to be humor, poked fun at the idea of enjoying a circus under any circumstances. In *Vanity Fair*, he joked that he went to a seance and asked, "Is the sperret [sic] of William Tompkins present?" When the spirit spoke to him through the medium, the "corn-pone humorist" was appalled to find that his dead friend had joined so dreadful a company of performers as a circus troupe.

Blissfully unaware of the low esteem in which every circus was held, the brothers from Iowa staged a road show in 1882. Al, oldest of the quintet, had become an accomplished tightrope walker and trapeze artist after having mastered the art of juggling. Because John, at age sixteen, gave such good performances as a clown and was already a good business manager, they made nearly one thousand dollars during the season. Still performing under their homemade tent, they traveled from town to town in nine farm wagons.

With cash in hand, the Ringlings were able to persuade veteran showman Yankee Robinson to let them team up with him. This alliance led to the Yankee Robinson and Ringling Brothers Great Double Shows, Circus, and Caravan that required a full dozen farm wagons for transport. Robinson soon died, so the young fellows from Iowa carried on without him and within three years had acquired a caravan of special wagons that were pulled by sixty horses.

Albert C. Ringling (1852–1916) was the first ringmaster of the enterprise launched by adolescents.—COURTESY OF JOHN AND MABEL RINGLING MUSEUM

In 1888, they acquired two elephants and made another name change to Ringling Brothers Greatest Show. They soon abandoned the use of wagons, except gilded ones designed for performances, and began moving their circus by rail. Largely under the skilled leadership of John, the youngest, the Ringlings added so many acts that by 1892, they required twenty-eight special railway cars. Except for The Greatest Show on Earth that had been launched by famous Phineas T. Barnum and later acquired by James Bailey, the Ringling circus had no close competitor.

John Ringling (1866–1936) had "the business head" among the five brothers and was not wiped out by the Great Depression despite losing millions because of it.—COURTESY OF JOHN AND MABEL RINGLING MUSEUM

Barnum & Bailey's show went to Europe in 1898 and spent five years there, so John and his brothers made the most of its absence. By the time The Greatest Show on Earth came back to the United States, the Ringlings had more than three hundred human performers, four times as many horses as Barnum & Bailey's show, an immense and varied menagerie, and a sideshow without equal. Claiming to having learned thrift from his German father, John went after small coins as well as large ones; he advertised chewing gum on the backs of posters and told his brothers—straight-faced—that from it "we are making a real wad."

Early in this century, the Ringlings bought 50 percent of the Forepaugh-Sells Circus and operated it so that it never opened in a city scheduled to be visited by Ringling Brothers. In 1907, they bought out their chief competitor, and with Barnum and Bailey added to its name after a decade, devotees of the ring agreed that the combined circus that traveled in 160 rail cars really was The Greatest Show on Earth. Europe and Asia were scouted for top riders and other performers; a particularly colorful equestrian was discovered in Australia and added to the Ringling lineup, which by then included the tight-rope walking Wallendas and clown Emmett Kelly as "Weary Willy."

Some analysts who have tried to account for the incredible success of five men who had little education and no training say that the Iowa work ethic and rule of honesty are central to the Ringling story. Each of the brothers really did work as hard as if he owned a small farm—and all of them scorned competitors who cheated or fleeced their patrons. At a time when more than a dozen other shows were on the road, only the Ringling Brothers ran hustlers and pickpockets off their lot. For years, an employee stationed close to the ticket wagon had a single function. Whenever a patron started away with tickets in hand, this fellow reminded him: "Don't leave until you have counted your change."

John Ringling took the family enterprise to Sarasota, Florida, and made investments that boosted him into the ranks of the twenty richest men in the world. He was toppled by the same set of uncontrollable factors that swept the ground from

Their "Magazine of Wonders," which sold for ten cents,
showed how much the five Ringlings resembled one another in
appearance.

under Herbert Hoover and led to the Great Depression. As a
result, the heirs of the five remarkable brothers lost control of
the entertainment empire that was conceived on the banks of
the Mississippi River when three tickets were given to an immigrant harness maker as a bonus for his work.

24
John Wayne

Swingin' Betsy

"What are your earliest vivid memories about?"

"Dust. Clouds of dust so thick a fella could hardly breathe," responded the veteran actor.

"How did you get into so much dust?"

"Ridin' the Chisholm Trail. I never came anywhere close to Abilene, though. Too far."

"I believe it must have been more than six hundred miles from Texas to the railhead in Kansas, so it's no wonder that you fell out along the way. How did you get from home to Texas in order to make the start?" a magazine writer inquired.

"Never got to Texas—except in my head; after all, I couldn't have been more'n about ten years old or maybe twelve."

"Was riding that trail in imagination your greatest boyhood adventure?"

"Nope. You asked about my earliest. My greatest adventure was in Texas—at the Alamo," Marion Robert Morrison responded.

"I suppose you also went to the Alamo in your imagination?"

"Sure. From somewhere or other, I got my hands on a beat-up old book about the Alamo. It had drawings of the place, and some of the men who fought there. The very first time I read that little book, I made up my mind that I'd spend a while there some day."

"Who was your favorite Alamo character?"

"Don't rightly know. Sometimes I was Bill Travis, a colonel and in charge of the whole place. There were days when I wouldn't answer when my mother called me until she yelled for Jim Bowie. Then I would come runnin' with a butcher knife in my hand. I guess I was Davy Crockett more than anybody

176

Wayne's portrayal of one-eyed Rooster Cogburn brought him an Academy Award.

else, though. Lots of times I picked up a long stick and made a rifle out of it. Then I grabbed it by the end of the barrel and beat the stuffin' out of a whole bunch of Mexicans."

"No wonder you had a lifelong ambition to make a film about the Alamo; now I understand why you were willing to sink a million of your own money into that project."

"It was over a million two and worth every cent of it because I got to play Davy Crockett," John Wayne (also known as Morrison) responded.

"I'm sure you got your money's worth, Duke. But you haven't told me how you got that name."

"It's a long story, but I'll try to make it short. When I got my first real job— delivering newspapers—my Airedale followed me around and stayed close to my heels. Nearly everybody on my route soon found out that the dog was named Duke. Some of them started joking about 'Little Duke and Big Duke'—the dog and me. Once that tag was put on me, it never fell off. I was mighty glad. It was no fun being called by a girl's name—Marion. That put the fellas to forever asking me why my mother dressed me in pants instead of a skirt."

John Wayne's memories of his boyhood, probably embellished during his years on Hollywood sets, were meager except for his imaginary adventures. After all, life in Winterset, Iowa, was humdrum for the most part. Even though the town was the seat of justice for Madison County, the biggest excitement there was the annual Fourth of July celebration. Clyde Morrison, the druggist who was Marion's father, never had a real-life encounter with a herd of cattle or a Mexican army. His mother, the former Mary Margaret Brown was a native of Ireland's County Cork. She gave Marion little time and attention after the birth of Robert Emmet, however.

"She always acted like Bobby had hung the moon," Duke recalled. "Even took away my middle name, gave it to my baby brother, and said I had to be Marion Michael from then on. My dad was a lot better; he didn't act like Bobby was an only child. He taught me one lesson I've never forgotten. 'Don't go lookin' for a fight,' he told me over and over, 'but if you get yourself into a fight, don't quit until you're damn sure you're the winner.'"

When Clyde began coughing a lot and sometimes spitting up blood, the family doctor told him to quit fighting the Iowa

As a youngster, the Duke imagined himself clad in buckskin and swinging his rifle, Betsy, at the Alamo.

climate and go to a hotter, drier place. So the entire family moved to a dreary eighty-acre spread on the rim of the Mojave Desert not far from Palmdale, California. They picked such a desolate place without running water and electricity because Clyde's father gave it to him. Having grown up in Iowa with such luxuries, Duke really missed them in California and never forgot the day in 1916 when his father came home and said they were moving into town where everybody had lights and water.

By the time he settled down in Glendale at age eleven, Duke wanted a job. He was glad to take a newspaper route, since that gave him a little spending money. "Fellas at the firehouse started the business of calling me Duke," he said long afterward. "My mother was too busy lookin' after Bobby to use that name, but I wouldn't answer to Marion and made her call me Jim or Davy a lot of the time."

Duke or Jim or Davy—or Marion—wanted to become an officer in the United States Navy but didn't have a high-placed friend to get him an appointment to the Naval Academy at Annapolis. So he went to the University of Southern California on an athletic scholarship and earned a letter in football. His scholarship didn't give him any cash, so he found a part-time job as propman at the Fox Film Corporation in Hollywood.

Availability, plus a height of six feet, four inches, and a photogenic face, landed him bit parts in a few movies—*Hangman's House*, *Salute*, *Men Without Women*, and *Rough Romance* (1928–30). He learned stunt riding from one of the best-known actors in early western films, Yakima Canutt, and he excelled at it. Director Raoul Walsh saw Duke in action and decided he was just right for a role in an expensive 1930 western. That's when he went through another name change. At Walsh's insistence the young actor became John Wayne to audiences who saw *The Big Trail* but continued to be Duke to his friends and fans.

Duke is remembered as the central figure of many Western movies. Yet during his appearances in more than two hundred films he assumed numerous roles. He was a seaman in *The Sea Spoilers* (1936), *The Long Voyage Home* (1940), and *The Wake of the Red Witch* (1948). He was a military figure in *Fort Apache* (1948),

*Wayne's enduring fame stems largely from
his many roles as a cow puncher.*

She Wore a Yellow Ribbon (1949), *The Sands of Iwo Jimo* (1949), *Rio
Grande* (1950), *Hondo* (1953), *The Green Berets* (1968), and *The
Undefeated* (1970). Duke was an airplane pilot in *The High and the
Mighty* (1954) and a Roman centurion in *The Greatest Story Ever
Told* (1965). He was a big game hunter in *Hatari!* (1962), then
extinguished oil field fires in *The Hellfighters* (1968). Few admirers remember that he appeared in at least two comedies that
were released a full generation apart—*No Reservations* (1946)
and *The War Wagon* (1967).

Regardless of his role, on screen John Wayne was almost
always himself—Big Duke. Bluff, hearty, forthright, daring, and
resourceful, he personified what he considered to be the best in
the American way of life. He once told a reporter that he didn't
have much use for his mother, but hated only one person—
communism founder Karl Marx.

A super patriot in the real sense of the word, the actor never
ran for office but consistently supported Republican candidates.
In 1964, he backed Barry Goldwater for president with such
ardor that he learned a campaign song and rendered it a few

times to small and select groups of intimates. Four years later he made a rare platform appearance by speaking at the Republican National Convention. To him, Richard M. Nixon was the greatest chief executive the nation ever had, so in 1972 he kept a pocket full of campaign buttons and handed them out to everyone he encountered.

Having drawn big money for years, in 1959, this hard-bitten two-fisted western hero decided to fulfill his childhood dream. He bankrolled the production of *The Alamo* and starred in it as Davy Crockett. To anyone who would listen he delivered a brief summary of his goal:

> We want to recreate a moment in history that will show this generation of Americans what their country really stands for. We want to show today's youngsters what their forebears went through to win what they had to have or die—liberty and freedom.

When his epic bombed among critics and at box offices, Wayne never complained that he had sunk an estimated 1.25 million dollars in it; he simply displayed the qualities that marked his performance as Rooster Cogburn in maybe the most appropriately named of his many films, *True Grit* (1969). His portrayal of that cantankerous leading character brought him the only Academy Award he ever won, though he was first nominated twenty years earlier.

As analyzed by noted critic Richard Schickel, the coveted award went to the Duke for his role as Rooster Cogburn, partly because of his personification of the best in the American way of life but also for his little-recognized ability to mingle subtle comedy with vigorous action. Schickel said of the 1969 release by Universal's leading man that:

> Wayne discovered what's funny about the character he has always played, and has now given the world an exuberant put-on that seems to delight him as much as it does us. *True Grit* represents, I think, the climax of a great and well-loved career both on the screen and as an American institution.

The "American institution" that was launched in the Hawk-eye State as Marion Morrison, then successively became the Duke and John Wayne, never indulged in posturing before cameras of news crews and refused to seek publicity. Year after year his name was in the *Motion Picture Herald*'s list of top ten money-makers in Hollywood, and he handled money as wisely as fame. Wayne bought and supervised ranches at Springerville and Stanfield, Arizona, and called a 135-foot yacht his only real indulgence. He lived for years at Newport Beach, California, in a home that cost him less than one-fourth of the money he poured into *The Alamo*. That movie was perhaps the poorest of all his major investments but was one he never regretted

Few motion picture stars of his magnitude have been more adamant about doing their own stunts. Danger meant nothing to the man from Winterset. He didn't want some "slick" stuntman standing in for him. This eagerness to do things right, and do them himself, was in keeping with the self-chosen epitaph of perhaps the most famous and admired of all actors who have considered westerns to be their genre. The Duke, who had a halting knowledge of spoken Spanish, said he wanted to be remembered only as *"Feo, fuerte, y formal"*—his personal rendition of "He may have been ugly, but he sure was strong and dignified."

The home where the Duke came into this world.—Courtesy of the Birthplace of John Wayne

25

Buddy Holly

The Day the Music Died

Four persons, three identified as nationally famous rock 'n' roll singers, died early Tuesday in a plane crash five miles north of Clear Lake.

The three singers were Buddy Holly, 22, Texas, Ritchie Valens, 21 [he was actually 17], Los Angeles, and J. P. Richardson, 24 [he was actually 28], of Louisiana, known professionally as the "Big Bopper."

Also killed was the pilot of the plane, Roger Peterson, 21, Clear Lake.

The entertainers had appeared at the Surf Ballroom Monday night and were to appear at Fargo, N.D., Tuesday night.

Other members of the troupe which appeared at Clear Lake left after the show by chartered bus for Fargo. They are Dion and the Belmonts, Frankie Sardo and the Crickets, of which Holly was the singing star.
—*Mason City Globe-Gazette*

Tragedy struck in the early morning of February 3, 1959, when three of rock 'n' roll's most creative and energetic entertainers were killed in a chartered airplane crash in an Iowa cornfield.

Ritchie Valens was one of the hottest recording stars in the United States. He was less than a year out of high school when he released a record with hits on both sides: "La Bamba," which had a Latin beat and lyrics, and "Donna," which had reached number four on the sales chart. Although his career lasted less than six months before he died, Valens had three hit songs, and according to his manager, "Everyone was calling him the next Elvis Presley."

J. P. Richardson, known as the "Big Bopper," was a singer/songwriter whose most famous song, "Chantilly Lace," was one he wrote and sang himself. The most enduring star to die that early Tuesday morning was Charles Hardin Holly from Lubbock, Texas. Although only twenty-two years old, Buddy Holly had written and performed a string of hits such as "That'll Be the Day," "Not Fade Away," "Well—All Right," and "Peggy Sue" and had appeared twice on the *Ed Sullivan Show*. Nearly fifty years after his death, Buddy Holly's music continues to live, and his innovations and influence have been widely recognized. He changed the face of popular music, specifically rock 'n' roll.

Waylon Jennings said, "it's almost impossible to listen to songs today or study the music of the most prominent artists of the past forty years and not hear the imprint of Buddy Holly." Holly was the first popular performer to overdub guitar and vocals to a recording. He was one of the first major artists to perform his own songs exclusively. Bill Griggs, who founded the Buddy Holly Memorial Society, said, "Buddy was one of the first musicians to do his recordings independent of the record company and proved that it was OK to wear glasses on stage." Griggs also said that Buddy Holly and the Crickets pioneered the "self-contained band," meaning that they did not heavily use studio musicians during recordings so that their sound was the same at live performances as on recordings, an innovation usually credited to the Beatles. Buddy Holly was also the first to use strings on a rock 'n' roll record and the first to use the combination of lead guitar, bass, rhythm guitar, and drums.

Don Everly of the Everly Brothers said, "Buddy was extremely talented, but he was very generous with that talent." Once in Florida, the Everly Brothers had to perform but did not have all their band members. Buddy backed them up for that show. "I think one of the reasons that other artists focus on Buddy Holly today," said Everly, "is that Buddy had his own unique sound and style…. There's something in Buddy's music that stirs the soul."

The Surf Ballroom in Clear Lake Iowa, was the last place Buddy Holly performed.
—COURTESY OF THE SURF BALLROOM. PHOTO BY JEFF HEINZ, *MASON CITY GLOBE-GAZETTE*

Mary Chapin Carpenter explained her feelings: "What is most striking about Buddy Holly's legacy is the combination of lyrical innocence and the redemptive power of his music. To this day they define what is magical to me about rock 'n' roll."

And Mike Harvey of *Super Gold* explained Buddy Holly's appeal:

"Buddy was one of the first of our generation—an actual teenager—to sit down and write songs about what we cared about. Buddy's songs were about experiences we all shared, which was unique at a time when most of the music was being written by 'adults.' Buddy knew our perspective. He knew the hot buttons to push and used the language and the terms we used every day. He wasn't glamorous like other teen stars of the time. He had a common look like the rest of us and a voice that we could all imitate. He was more one of us than anyone else."

Buddy Holly was born on September 7, 1936, in Lubbock, Texas. He began taking violin lessons when he was eight years

old, and seven years later he changed to guitar. He began
singing and playing at various clubs in the Southwest, and
while still in high school, he and a friend named Jack Neal had
their own radio show: *The Buddy and Jack Show.* He graduated
from Lubbock High School in 1955. Then, he made some
recordings in a studio in Clovis, New Mexico, owned by Norman Petty, who took Buddy's demonstration record to Murry
Deutsch of the Southern Music Publishing Company in New
York. Deutsch, in turn, took it to Bob Thiel of Carol and
Brunswick Records, a subsidiary of Decca, and Brunswick
signed Buddy and the Crickets, a group Buddy had formed in
Lubbock, to a recording contract. Impresario Irvin Feld then
signed them for the "Biggest Show of Stars for '57." In September 1957, "That'll Be the Day" hit number one and brought
Buddy Holly and the Crickets world-wide attention. By Octo-
ber 1, 1957, the song had sold one million copies.

Buddy got more than just a recording contract from his contact at Southern Music Publishing. An executive there had a
niece who had moved to New York from Puerto Rico when she
was ten. The niece, Maria Elena, met Buddy through her aunt
and put her plans to be an actress and a dancer on hold to
marry Buddy Holly.

Buddy Holly and the Crickets toured from September
through November 1957 and were a hit. In December, they were
in New York City to appear on the Ed Sullivan Show and met
Jerry Lee Lewis. After the new year, Lewis, Paul Anka, Buddy
Holly, and the Crickets toured Hawaii and Australia, where
they performed in Melbourne, Sydney, and Brisbane. They continued to tour throughout 1958 until Buddy decided to move to
New York to become involved in the business side of music.
Drummer J. I. Allison and bassist Joe B. Mauldin made a deal to
keep the Crickets' name and recorded albums on their own
without Buddy. The biggest hit Buddy and the Crickets had was
"Peggy Sue," which sold more than 1.5 million copies.

In the 1950s most popular bands went on exhausting road
trips of one-night performances in school gyms, roller rinks,
armories, and ballrooms. In February of 1959, a grueling two-
week Winter Dance Party tour consisting of Ritchie Valens, The

One of the most popular bands of the time, The Crickets—especially Buddy Holly—influenced countless musicians, even inspiring the Beatles' name.—COURTESY OF THE SURF BALLROOM

Big Bopper, and Buddy Holly was put together by General Artists of Chicago. One of the band members was an unknown guitar player named Waylon Jennings.

The Surf Ballroom in Clear Lake was built in 1933. Whether big band, country, polka, or rock, the music and dancing at the Surf Ballroom was always unforgettable. On Monday, February 2, 1959, more than a thousand fans packed the dance floor at $1.25 each to enjoy the music and dance. "The entertainers were full of pep, reacting joyously to the big crowd of young people," reported *The Clear Lake Mirror Reporter*. "The 'Big Bopper' and Ritchie Valens playfully Indian wrestled backstage between acts." After the concert, Buddy called Maria Elena, his wife, to let her know how the tour was going.

The next concert was to be in Moorehead, Minnesota. The touring bus had experienced some mechanical problems and had almost no heat, and so a plane was chartered to fly part of the group to Fargo, North Dakota, the closest airport to Moorhead, to make advance preparations and get their shirts laundered before the next concert. It was decided at the last minute exactly who should go on the plane. The Big Bopper got a seat on the plane because he had the flu. Waylon Jennings and Ritchie Valens tossed a coin, and Valens got to go on the plane. Buddy Holly joked with Jennings that he hoped the bus would break down. Jennings then joked back, saying that he hoped the plane would crash, a comment he has had to live with ever since.

The single-engine, four-seater Beechcraft Bonanaza left the Mason City Municipal Airport shortly after 1 A.M. on February 3. The trip should have taken about three and a half hours. When the plane did not arrive on time, the owner began to look for the Beechcraft, but his search was delayed by early morning fog. The *Mason City Globe-Gazette* described what he found:

> It was obvious that the pilot had been flying on a straight northwest line and was at a very low angle to the ground when he hit…. The left wing of the plane seemingly struck the ground and plowed a furrow for about a dozen feet before it crumpled and the body of the plane hit. It dug a shallow depression in the stubble field and the wing fell off as the rest of the plane bounced. It struck the ground again about 50 feet farther northwest and then skidded on the ground about two city blocks until it piled up against a fence. The wreckage was a jumbled mass, which would not have been recognized as a plane. Along the skid path small bits of the plane and its contents were strewn. There was a man's shoe, a traveling bag and small pieces of the plane, including parts of the instrument panel. The bag was the largest piece except for the wing, the jumble against the fence, and three bodies…. Authorities do not yet know the cause of the accident. Some believe, however, that ice may have formed on the wings or windshield making a forced landing necessary.

The concert in Moorehead did go on, but with other artists who volunteered: Bill Haley and the Comets, Bill Parsons, and

The wreckage of the plane that carried Buddy Holly, Ritchie Valens, and J. P. Richardson (the "Big Bopper").—COURTESY OF SURF BALLROOM. PHOTO BY ELWIN MUSSER, *MASON CITY GLOBE-GAZETTE*

Frankie Avalon. Local performer Bobbie Vee, who later charted thirty-eight songs on Billboard's top ten, and his brother Bill also performed.

The influence of Buddy Holly and the Crickets on the world of popular music can hardly be overstated. The first song John Lennon and George Harrison learned to play was "That'll Be the Day," and the name *Crickets* even inspired the Beatles' name.

"There's a kind of mystique to dying young," said Don Everly. "Buddy's death was the result of the kind of pressure we all had at the time. When you get right down to it, his death was so unnecessary. The bottom line is, he was just struggling to get his laundry done. That's why he was flying."

J. I. Allison, drummer for the Crickets, explained that Buddy Holly put more of an emphasis on the music than on the artist's appearance in determining rock 'n' roll popularity. "We opened the door for other musicians based on their talent. I've always said that Buddy killed the 'pretty boy' image of rock 'n' roll by being the first ugly guy to make it big, although he really wasn't ugly. What I mean is that Buddy proved you didn't have to be a teen idol with a whole lot of press or glossy photos to make it big."

Mike Harvey said, "Buddy was never considered a true superstar when he was alive and that's because his recording label did not know how to distribute or promote a star of his caliber. If you look at his body of work, there were dozens of songs that were never hits because the record company either didn't record, release, or promote what he did. It's criminal how badly Buddy Holly's work was handled at the time."

If he had lived, Holly would probably have become a major force in the music industry. Just before he died he had purchased property in Lubbock where he wanted to build a recording studio. He wanted to write scores for movies and a piece for a philharmonic orchestra. "It was always very important to Buddy to not be boring," said Maria Elena Holly. "He always wanted to get somewhere and be remembered."

Holly is probably more widely known today than he was when he died. In 1978, Gary Busey starred in *The Buddy Holly Story*. And every February about two thousand people go to Clear Lake, Iowa, from all over the world to pay homage to Buddy at an annual tribute at the Surf Ballroom.

26
Johnny Carson

Young Pretender

Neighborhood youngsters who gathered on the porch at 725 Cherry Street near the East Nishnabotna River nudged one another and grinned. They had come for lemonade plus a free performance by a friend, but they were primed to voice disappointment and disgust. When The Great Carsoni made his appearance through the front door of his home, his improvised cape startled them so much that they forgot to shout "Boo!" at the top of their lungs.

Believe it or not, boys and girls of Avoca, Iowa, actually yelled their approval when their new friend who had come from Red Oak finished his performance and gave a bow. At an early age he was dying to perform magic tricks. A mail-order course in ventriloquism and long hours of practice paid off when the young Johnny Carson became known as The Young Houdini.

Years later, he remembered feeling a sudden and unexpected surge of energy the minute he knew he had his audience in the palm of his hand. Experienced countless times during his career, he described the feeling as a powerful "high," a "strange feeling" that he never fully understood. "I don't think you can get it from drugs," he said. "I doubt that it comes from anything else [except audience reactions]. Your mind starts to let you do things you didn't even realize you could do."

Even his closest blood relatives say that family tradition fails to indicate precisely when John William Carson started pretending. Born on Main Street in Corning, the youngster was taken by his family to Clarinda very early and from there to Red Oak. By the time the Carsons were well settled in Red Oak,

191

By the time he graduated from the University of Nebraska at Lincoln, the young fellow from Iowa was noted as being willing to do anything for a laugh.—UNIVERSITY OF NEBRASKA

Johnny was old enough to go to kindergarten. He had hardly begun to get acquainted with the other kids before his father, who was a manager for the Iowa and Nebraska Power and Light Company, got another promotion that required him to move again, to Avoca, nearly fifty miles away.

Avoca is central to Johnny's earliest memories, but he didn't get a chance to grow up there. Despite the strong Iowa roots of his father and mother—Logan and Bedford, respectively—Logan ("Kit") Carson couldn't pass up a chance to become an office manager for his company. This promotion took the family to Norfolk, Nebraska, where Johnny spent his adolescent years.

The Great Carsoni, whose early interest in magic dulled due to the hours he spent with a console radio that brought *The Jack Benny Show* to Kit's home, was not impressed when he was told that three railroads ran through Norfolk. He was a whole lot more interested in *Fibber McGee and Molly* than in the Chicago, St. Paul & Omaha or even the Union Pacific and the Northwestern.

Musing about his boyhood and trying to analyze himself as a professional entertainer, Carson told a reporter that he believed he must have been "a sorta shy kid who found out he could get up in front of a bunch of fellows and get their attention by doing or saying something different." When he became a minor campus notable at the University of Nebraska in Lincoln, a history teacher reputedly arrived at a similar conclusion.

"Carson," he is quoted as having said, "has some kind of inner urge that makes him want to take the place of a big-name entertainer." Borrowing from the terminology of monarchs, the teacher compared the student with men who wanted to topple their king in order to assume the throne. "Johnny," he said, "is 'The Young Pretender' who wants to unseat Will Rogers and become king of laughs."

If that verdict is remembered accurately, it was almost prophetic when delivered soon after the end of World War II. At the start of that global conflict, Johnny was holding down his first real job—you might have guessed that it would be at the Granada

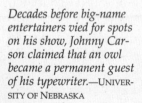

Decades before big-name entertainers vied for spots on his show, Johnny Carson claimed that an owl became a permanent guest of his typewriter.—UNIVERSITY OF NEBRASKA

Theatre in Norfolk. When he finished high school he was inducted into the U.S. Navy, so he often entertained men aboard the USS *Pennsylvania* before entering college. In Lincoln, he wangled his first media job and wrote a comic western for radio station KFAB. As a university senior he penned a thesis; perhaps you can guess its subject if not its name—"Comedy Writing."

Still considered by some who encountered him as "wet behind the ears," the graduate worked at radio station WOW in Omaha before moving to KNX-TV in Los Angeles. Management at the latter station gave him a shot at a half-hour comedy show on Sunday afternoon, and through it he caught the attention of Groucho Marx and Red Skelton.

Skelton soon made him a member of the staff responsible for writing his CBS-TV show, and the network later put *The Johnny Carson Show* on the air. It bombed but limped along for thirty-nine weeks; when the final episode was aired, the Iowa native headed to the Big Apple and at age thirty-two was seen every week as host of an ABC quiz show, *Who Do You Trust?* Toward the latter part of the five years the show stayed on the air, Johnny was Jack Paar's regular guest on the *Tonight Show*.

When Paar finally acted upon his frequent threat to quit, Johnny took over after an interval of six months. This move meant boarding a sinking ship, for the audience and revenue of the *Tonight Show* were going down like a warship that had been hit by a torpedo. Black-and-white television sets did not reveal the almond-shaped eyes of the host that were an unusual shade of hazel. But his deadpan humor plus his unfailing readiness to let guests seem to upstage him soon started the show toward the top of the charts.

At age forty-two, the Corning native was the subject of a cover story in *Time* magazine. Lauded as "an institution," he was credited with having made the *Tonight Show* the biggest moneymaker in television history. By 1972, when he moved the show from New York to Hollywood, the fellow who started as The Great Carsoni in front of a handful of neighborhood kids was performing for nightly audiences of more than fifteen million.

To the consternation of his nationwide following, Kit Carson's son threatened to quit while on top. He announced in

Johnny's famous look of blank surprise was flashed in Lincoln, when he returned for a football game in 1971.

April 1979 that he would leave the *Tonight Show* a year before expiration of his contract, which reportedly brought him three million dollars a year. He changed his mind, however, and stayed on the air until 1992. His change of heart was probably due to new terms that gave him more time off and a big raise.

Off camera, he is still like the youngster who got up in front of audiences to conceal his shyness. Writing in *Look* magazine, Betty Rollin penned what may be the best-ever description of Carson. "Off-camera," she wrote, "Johnny is testy, defensive, withdrawn and wonderfully inept, and uncomfortable with people."

By then he no longer had to pretend to be the King of Comedy. Depending upon who was talking or writing about him, he had become the "Mark Twain of Talk," the "Will Rogers of Television," or "America's Clown Prince" and no longer needed to worry about what people might think of him.

Bibliography

Adams, James Truslow, ed. *Album of American History*. 5 vols. New York: Scribner's, 1945.

Alderman, Clifford L. *Osceola and the Seminole Wars*. New York: Messner, 1973.

Allen, Lee and Tom Meany. *Kings of the Diamond*. N.Y: Putnam, 1965.

American Goliath, The. Syracuse: n.p, 1869.

American Heritage Pictorial History of the Presidents of the United States. 2 vols. New York: American Heritage, 1968.

American Image, The. Photographs from the National Archives. New York: Random House, 1979.

The American West. Pleasantville: Reader's Digest Assoc., 1978.

Armstrong, Perry A. *The Sauks and the Black Hawk War*. New York: AMS Press reprint, 1979.

Aumann, F. F. "The Watchful Fox." *The Palimpsest* (April 1928).

Barzman, Sol. *The First Ladies*. New York: Cowles, 1970.

The Baseball Hall of Fame 50th Anniversary. New York: Prentice Hall, 1988.

Black Hawk. *Life of Ma-ka-tai-me-she-kia-kiak*. Cincinnati: n.p., 1833.

Blassingame, Wyatt. *Osceola*. Champaign: Garrard, 1967.

Boller, Paul F., Jr. *Presidential Wives*. New York: Oxford University Press, 1988.

Bryan, Conn. *Confederate Georgia*. Athens: University of Georgia Press, 1953.

Buchanan, Lamont. *The World Series*. New York: Dutton, 1951.

Cardiff Giant Humbug, The. Fort Dodge: n.p, 1870.

Century Magazine, October 1902.

Collins, Alan C. *The Story of America in Pictures*. Rev ed. Garden City: Doubleday, 1953.

Cruikshank, Ernest A. "The Employment of Indians in the War of 1812." *Report of the American Historical Association*, 1895, pp. 321–35.

Current Biography, 1940.

D'Aulaire, Ingri and Edgar D'Aulaire. *Buffalo Bill*. Garden City: Doubleday, 1952.

Degregorio, William A. *The Complete Book of U.S. Presidents*. New York: Wings, 1993.

Dickey, Glenn. *The History of American League Baseball*. New York: Stein & Day, 1982.

Dodge, Grenville M. "Recollections." *New York MOLLUS*. Wilmington: Broadfoot reprint, 1995.

————, *Personal Recollections*. Council Bluffs: n.p., 1911.

Donaldson, Thomas. "The Catlin Indian Gallery" in *Smithsonian Institute Annual Report of 1885*.

Dubofsky, Melvyn and Warren Van Tine. *John L. Lewis*. New York: New York Times, 1977.

Dupuy, Tevor N. et al. *Harper Encyclopedia of Military Biography*. New York: HarperCollins, 1992.

Eaton, Clement. *Jefferson Davis*. New York: Free Press, 1977.

Einstein, Charles, ed. *The Fireside Book of Baseball*. New York: Simon and Schuster, 1956.

Embree, Edwin R. *Thirteen Against the Odds*. New York: Viking, 1944.

Fairall, Herbert S. *The Iowa Masonic Library*. Cedar Rapids: n.p., 1899.

Faust, Patricia L, ed. *Historical Times Illustrated Encyclopedia of the Civil War*. New York: Harper & Row, 1986.

Forbis, William H. *The Cowboys*. Alexandria: Time Life, 1973.

Frank, Beryl. *Pictorial History of the Republican Party*. New York: Castle, 1980.

The Freemason and the Fez (Cedar Rapids), May 1895.

The Freemason Chronicle (London), August 1876.

Galloway, John D. *The First Transcontinental Railroad*. New York: Simmons-Boardman, 1950.

Garst, Shannon. *The Story of Buffalo Bill*. Indianapolis: Bobbs-Merrill, 1938

Goodwin, Doris K. *No Ordinary Time*. New York: Simon & Schuster, 1994.

The Great American West. Pleasantville: Reader's Digest, 1977.

Gurko, Miriam. *Indian America: The Black Hawk War*. New York: Crowell, 1970.

Gurney, Gene. *Pictorial History of the U. S. Army.* New York: Crown, 1972.

Haley, Alex. *The Playboy Interviews* (Johnny Carson). New York: Ballantine, 1993.

Hamilton, Holman. "Zachary Taylor and the Black Hawk War." *Wisconsin Magazine of History* 24 (1941), pp. 305–15.

Harper's Encyclopedia of United States History. 10 vols. New York: Harper & Bros., 1905.

Hartley, William and Ellen Hartley. *Osceola.* New York: Hawthorn, 1973.

Herbert Hoover: An American Epic. Vol. II. Chicago: Regnery, 1960.

Hering, Daniel W. *Foibles and Fallacies of Science.* New York: Van Nostrand, 1924.

Hirshson, Stanley P. *Grenville M. Dodge.* Bloomington: University of Indiana Press, 1967.

Hodge, Frederick W., ed. *Handbook of American Indians North of Mexico.* 2 vols. Washington: Bureau of American Ethnology, 1907–10.

Holbrook, Stewart H. *The Story of American Railroads.* New York: Crown, 1947.

Holt, Rackham. *Carver.* Garden City: Doubleday, Doran, 1943.

Honig, Donald. *The Chicago Cubs.* New York: Prentice Hall, 1991.

Howard, Robert W. *The Great Iron Trail.* New York: Putnam, 1962.

Hutchinson Dictionary of Biography. London: Helicon, 1993.

Ithaca Daily Journal, January 1898.

Johnson, Allen. *Dictionary of American Biography.* 29 vols. New York: Scribner's, 1929–46.

Johnson, R. P. *Osceola.* Minneapolis: Dillon, 1973.

Kaplan, Justin. *Mr. Clemens and Mark Twain.* New York: Simon & Schuster, 1966.

Leamer, Laurence. *King of the Night—Johnny Carson.* New York: Morrow, 1989.

Lewis, Oscar. *The Big Four.* New York: Knopf, 1938.

Lipscomb, Shirley and George D. Lipscomb. *Dr. George Washington Carver.* New York: Messner, 1983.

Life, January 23, 1970.

Lorant, Stefan. *The Presidency*. New York: Macmillan, 1951.

McElroy, Robert. *Jefferson Davis*. New York: Smithmark, reprint 1995.

McHenry, Robert, ed. *Famous American Women*. New York: Dover reprint, 1983.

———, *Webster's American Military Biographies*. New York: Dover, 1978.

McMurry, Linda O. *George Washington Carver*. New York: Oxford University Press, 1981.

Marlow, Joan. *The Great Women*. New York: Galahad, 1979.

Mathews, Mitford M. *A Dictionary of Americanisms*. 2 vols. Chicago: University of Chicago Press, 1957.

Meltzer, Milton. *Mark Twain Himself*. New York: Bonanza, 1940.

Milner, Clyde A, II, et al., eds. *The American West*. New York: Oxford University Press, 1994.

Mulder, William and A. Russell Mortensen, eds. *Among the Mormons*. New York: Knopf, 1958.

New Albany Ledger, July 21, 1864.

New York State Historical Association, Special Collections.

New York Tribune, July 21, 1864.

New York Commercial Appeal, July 23, 1864.

Niles' National Register, October 1837.

Osceola. Osceola, Neb.: Centennial Book Committee, 1972.

Ploski, Harry A., ed. *The Negro Almanac*. New York: Wiley, 1983.

Polley, Robert L., gen. ed. *Folk Art*. Waukesha, Wis.: Country Beautiful, 1941.

Popular Science Monthly, June 1878.

Quaife, Milo Milton, ed. *The Southwestern Expedition of Zebulon M. Pike*. Chicago: Donnelley, 1925.

Reichler, Joseph L. *The Great All-time Baseball Record Book*. New York: Macmillan, l981.

Roberts, Randy, and James S. Olson. *John Wayne*. New York: Free Press, 1995.

Rosa, Joseph G. and Robin May. *Buffalo Bill*. Lawrence: University of Kansas Press, 1989.

Russell, Don. *Buffalo Bill*. Norman: University of Oklahoma Press, 1960.

Sage, Leland L. *A History of Iowa*. Ames: Iowa State University Press, 1974.

Seale, William. *The President's House*. 2 vols. Washington: White House Historical Association, 1986.

Shebar, Sharon. *The Cardiff Giant*. New York: Messner, 1983.

Smart Set, June 1919.

Smith, Robert. *Illustrated History of Baseball*. New York: Grossett & Dunlap, 1973.

Stegner. *The Gathering of Zion*. New York: McGraw-Hill, 1964.

Stewart, Gail B. *Famous Hoaxes*. New York: Crestwood, 1990.

Syme, Ronald. *Osceola*. New York: Morrow, 1976.

Taylor, Tim. *The Book of Presidents*. New York: Arno, 1972.

Terrell, John U. *Zebulon Pike*. New York: Weybright and Talley, 1968.

Upson, Theodore F. *With Sherman to the Sea*. Bloomington: Indiana University Press, 1943.

Van der Zee, Jacob. "The Black Hawk War and the Treaty of 1832," *Iowa Journal of History and Politics*, July 1915.

Wall, Joseph F. *Iowa—A History*. New York: Norton, 1978.

War of the Rebellion, Official Records, Serial Nos. 74, 76. Washington: Government Printing Office, 1891.

Warren, Ruth. *A Pictorial History of Women in America*. New York: Crown, 1975.

Wayne, Pilar. *John Wayne*. New York: McGraw-Hill, 1987.

Weatherford, Doris. *American Women's History*. New York: Prentice Hall, 1994.

Weatherford, Jack. *Indian Givers*. New York: Crown, 1988.

Whitney, Ellen M., comp. *The Black Hawk War*.

Index

Boldface page numbers indicate illustrations.